BREAKWATER

Poems

Also by Catharine Savage Brosman

POETRY

Watering (Athens: University of Georgia Press, 1972)
Abiding Winter (Florence, Ky: R. L. Barth, 1983) [chapbook]
Journeying from Canyon de Chelly (Baton Rouge: LSU Press, 1990)
Passages (Baton Rouge: LSU Press, 1996)
The Swimmer and Other Poems (Edgewood, Ky: R. L. Barth, 2000) [chapbook]
Places in Mind (Baton Rouge: LSU Press, 2000)
Petroglyphs: Poems and Prose (Thibodaux, La: Jubilee: A Festival of the Arts,
        Nicholls State University, 2003) [chapbook]
The Muscled Truce (Baton Rouge: LSU Press, 2003)
Range of Light (Baton Rouge: LSU Press, 2007)

CREATIVE PROSE

The Shimmering Maya and Other Essays (Baton Rouge: LSU Press, 1994)
Finding Higher Ground: A Life of Travels (Reno: University of Nevada Press, 2003)

CRITICISM

André Gide: l'évolution de sa pensée religieuse (Paris: Nizet, 1962)
Malraux, Sartre, and Aragon as Political Novelists (Gainesville: University of Florida
        Press, 1964)
Roger Martin du Gard (New York: Twayne Publishers, 1968)
Jean-Paul Sartre (Boston: Twayne Publishers, 1983)
Jules Roy (Philadelphia: Celfan Edition Monographs, 1988)
An Annotated Bibliography of Criticism on André Gide, 1973-1988 (New York:
        Garland, 1990)
Simone de Beauvoir Revisited (Boston: Twayne, 1991)
Twentieth-Century French Culture, 1900-1975, edited with an introduction
        (Detroit: Gale, 1995)
Visions of War in France: Fiction, Art, Ideology (Baton Rouge: LSU Press, 1999)
Existential Fiction (Detroit: Gale, 2000)
Albert Camus (Detroit: Gale, 2000)

BREAKWATER

Poems

Catharine Savage Brosman

MERCER UNIVERSITY PRESS
MACON, GEORGIA

MUP/P391

© 2009 Mercer University Press
1400 Coleman Avenue
Macon, Georgia 31207

First Edition.

Books published by Mercer University Press are printed on acid free paper that meets the requirements of American National Standard for Information Sciences—Permanence of Paper for Printed Library Materials.

Mercer University Press is a member of Green Press initiative (greenpressinitiative.org), a nonprofit organization working to help publishers and printers increase their use of recycled paper and decrease their use of fiber derived from endangered forests. This book is printed on recycled paper.

Library of Congress Cataloging-in-Publication Data
Brosman, Catharine Savage, 1934-
Breakwater : poems / Catharine Savage Brosman. -- 1st ed. p. cm.
ISBN-13: 978-0-88146-180-0 (hardback : alk. paper)
ISBN-10: 0-88146-180-6 (hardback : alk. paper)
ISBN-13: 978-0-88146-163-3 (pbk. : alk. paper)
ISBN-10: 0-88146-163-6 (pbk. : alk. paper) I. Title.
PS3552.R666B74   2009
811'.54--dc22
2009004533

This book is for Patric Savage,
once and now again my husband—
with gratitude, admiration, and love;
and also for Katherine Brosman Deimling,
my darling daughter.

Contents

Acknowledgments

Grateful acknowledgment is made to the publishers of the following magazines and anthologies, where the poems mentioned first appeared: *Bulletin des Amis d'André Gide*: "Madeleine Gide in Algeria"; *Burning Light*: "Chimayo"; *Le Cerf-Volant*: "Birds in the Bush"; *Chronicles: A Magazine of American Culture*: "Saint-Séverin, I"; *First Things*: "Saint-Séverin, II"; *Louisiana Literature*: "In Unaweep Canyon"; *Magnolia Quarterly*: "Desire"; *Měasure*: "Bougainvillea: An Epithalamium," "Fire in the Mind;" "Pike's Peak: October"; "The Trout"; *Modern Age*: "Vaux-le-Vicomte"; *Pennsylvania Review* (an on-line magazine): "By the Conejos River," "Shadow," "To Former Students, Who Would Be Skeptical"; *Sewanee Review*: "Burning in Louvain," "Carafes," "D. H. Lawrence in the Hopi Lands," "Flying Straight," "Fortune's Choice," "Marmalade," "Mina Loy in Mexico"; *Sewanee Theological Review*: "Fire Ring"; *Smartish Pace*: "On the Bayou"; *South Carolina Review*: "By the Black Canyon of the Gunnison," "Carnations." Two of the Pernette translations appeared in *Měasure*: others were published by *The New Formalist* (an on-line magazine). "Butterflies All of One Dark" appeared originally in my chapbook *Abiding Winter* (Florence KY: R. L. Barth, 1983), and was republished in *Poetry Calendar for 2005* (Bertem, Belgium: Alhambra Publishers, 2004). "Christ Pantokrator" was published in *Points of Gold: Poems for Leo Luke Marcello*, Stella Nesanovich, ed. (New Orleans: Xavier University Press, 2005) and was republished in *Modern Age*. "Burning in Louvain" was republished in *Dramatic Monologues: A Contemporary Anthology*, Samuel Maio, ed. (Evansville: University of Evansville Press, 2009). Two poems appeared also in French translation by Jeannine Hayat, one in the *Bulletin des Amis d'André Gide*: "Madeleine Gide en Algérie," the other in *Le Cerf-Volant*: "Comme l'oiseau sur la branche."

To Her Book

As Orpheus reaped music with his lyre,
your pages, ripened, harvested in sheaves
well-bound beneath late summer moons on fire,
ride out on tourbillons with live oak leaves.

They'll take their chance—a toy boat in a stream
rain-swollen, torn on rapids or fast-whirled
in eddies, trapped by branches' damming scheme—
impassive, tangled image of the world;

or—kites that sail on an auspicious wind—
they'll find a tethered welcome, adding fact
to promise. Not a line should you rescind,
respectful of the literary pact.

Farewell, then. May your readers be those birds
which by an Orphic song were freely caught,
embracing as their own the poet's words,
the very shape and countenance of thought.

I

Breakwater*

No man's an island, maybe, but this hump of concrete,
breaching the swirling current like a whale,
is one. It's just downstream from a breakwater
formed of pilings at the confluence of two urban bayous—
one, flowing in disguise beneath a park and roads,
then surfacing—a memory that comes to mind;

the other, Bray's Bayou—swift thought from the west.
The pilings shape the confrontation—elbowing
the water as it passes, eddies, rushes onward, then divides
at the island prow. All this belonging to the city's
body. Here too are ducks, bobbing in the turbulence,
living flotsam—going under, reappearing;

another on the island preens and spreads his wings
as if in admiration. By the edge stand two blue herons,
both *habitués*, I judge, and unperturbed, apparently.
In love, beside the man who was my husband
long ago, I gaze with them, scanning the stream. Strange:
my middle decades—Dante's tangled wood—appear

a foreign thing, lived by someone else. Yet that was *I*.
Now, having passed the breakwater, we've landed
on this island of our age, two Robinsons, conjoined,
and canopied by trees whose million leaves
murmur love of light and lucid shade, and paint
the bayou in great shimmering mottles, figuring happiness.

——

* Notes on this and other poems will be found at the end of part three.

A Colorado Suite

1: In the Hayman Burn

What profusion of wild flowers in hues of fire bloom
this summer—scarlet gilia, blue harebells, yellow
cinquefoil, Queen Anne's lace—where flames
of the same incandescent colors took a forest down—
the grass scorched first, the very ground

exhausted, aspen, pines, and fir, in green armadas
on the waving hillsides, stripped and charred,
their skeletons erect still, useless masts, or fallen,
driftwood, in the wreckage. It was all (she said)
to burn a letter in a campfire. That year, the drought,

a vampire, had prowled the mountains greedily,
drying up the springs and creeks and sucking
trees with hot, consuming breath. The man she loved
had not responded as she'd wished; and so
his image had to be destroyed. Who hasn't wished

to turn a memory to smoke? To wipe a moment,
or another being, from the world, to prove that love
is merely ash and air, by altering its tokens
in consuming chemistry, because one cannot change
oneself, or undo time, where thoughts are wisps

of nothingness, just little tropisms, but acts are stones.
Today the air is clear; the snows of recent winters
and the patient seeds have bored through soil,
and rains this season, generous with drops
of succulence, have also washed out death, as tears

long-distilled relieve regret. I do not have another fifty
years; I've got to take the forest as it is, half-
ruined, wishing things redone, imagining green life,
young trees, a chance to kindle a new fire in the heart—
catching, glowing steadily, burning without loss.

2: By the Black Canyon of the Gunnison

This is the place where one could cast it all
in the abyss—the selfishness and pride,
the casual indifference, or just
oneself. Two aging bikers stop—a man,

a woman—cut their engines, and resume,
before they even look around, the quarrel
they gave up briefly on the road. It makes
me turn away in shame for those who waste

their love. A stone dislodged slips slowly down,
then by its own momentum frees itself
and plunges through the scraggly juniper
along the cliff side, pinging boulders high

above the river, then descending, deep
and finally invisible, at rest,
perhaps with grass that pearls along the slope,
or in the water's sinuous, green truth.

No fall can free me thus, not even death,
from the morass of acts, a tangled net
cast retrospectively. The only way
goes past the drop-off, upwards, toward the blue

San Juans, in sunlight, and Grand Mesa's prow,
which tacks among the clouds and sweeps its way
across, proposing new departures, knots
cut through, great roadsteads, and immense desires.

3: In Unaweep Canyon

Crossing the Gunnison, we bounced along a small plateau,
gray and scruffy with its sagebrush, then drove up
through badlands, tangled like *chevaux de frise*,
to the aspen and dark conifers—spruce, pine, and fir—
of a glaciated valley in the Uncompahgre Forest. Looking

even, trimmed, the slopes might pass for fairways, lifted
when the earth turned over, shrugged its shoulders,
scattered boulders to all sides to make the rough
and bunkers, later graded steeply by the ice. To be sure,
that smoothness is deceptive, like so many other

first impressions. Now we've reached the canyon country,
stark, where the Dolores River and its confluents
carved out ravines, and winds well-forged eroded
remnants of the mesa, leaving mostly space. What green
survives here comes from cottonwoods and willows

near the river, isolated piñon pines and juniper, young hay
in bottomlands; all the rest is rock, of rose and coral,
flaming on the canyon sides, fallen at the angle
of repose down jagged taluses, rising in palisades
that wall the heights. Above, unblemished blue unfurls

its tent for the deep-channeled earth. How whole this is,
how unified, with all its contrasts and sharp salience—
cubist blocks in disarray, swift water, sandstone
pillars in the sky, and precipitous inclines of velvet
forest. It's the beauty of conciliation, something eye

→

and mind can do with shards and pieces of a life, a world—
half-artisan, half-god, refining, shaping matter
into meaning, gathering lines of force that seemed
irreparably bent apart, composing them into a sheaf
of purpose, modulating strange desires by common chords.

4: By the Conejos River

The water, high for autumn, carries thought
downstream past grassy banks and fallen trees,
through weirs of river stones and branches, caught
like rough objections to a fluid ease.

It's not pellucid, nor the mind's ideal—
or is it? Obstacles can make us wise;
perfection may be gauged by how you feel,
as beauty's proven in beholders' eyes.

I step into the river, running swift
and frothy, swirling, magnified by light;
it's buoyant, though, providing flow and lift,
resistance furnishing the greater height.

And now I think my heart's contrary moods—
each eddying pool, dark current, headstrong act—
aren't merely detours and vicissitudes,
but purchase for a leaping, muscled pact.

5: Wilkerson Pass

Threading my way west beyond the redrock narrows
of Cascade, over Ute Pass, into Park County,
through sage and venerable '30s pines, I'm rising
towards the crest called Wilkerson, which leads down
to South Park. All the way my mind has been on you,
remembering our campsites in the high desert
of Wyoming, off a gravel track, far from anything—
just brush and juniper—and in Montana, where a bear

nosed round us in the night; recalling, too, New Mexico
and how after a monsoon rain our Chevrolet
got deeply mired on a gravel road. —It's solitude
that brings back all these memories, and the elevation—
climbing, climbing through the bends, reaching
the altitude of ponderosas and the aspen groves,
girlish, gowned in white, heads fluttering. As I hit
the summit, look across the basin, waving blue below,

and gaze toward the Mosquito Range, northwest,
and west to the Collegiates, what moves me even more
to think of you with joy is space—as if constrictions
of the years were loosened suddenly—a weir unlocked,
a liberated heart—with all this sky flying above me
on its cirrus wings that brush the distance,
and the prospect, smooth, of undulating sagebrush
stretching north to Fairplay, southward to the creeks

and bayous that sustain Eleven Mile Reservoir. Here,
two forks of the South Platte meander, looping,
almost hidden by lush grass and willows. Though
the summer's gone, the river rushes, swift, after early
snows and fat-dropped rains. Descending now
on switchbacks, the perspective changing, I can put
the views together, see the whole, a lifetime.
I've come around: the circle's widened, but the center

holds: in these latter years, I live in Colorado, dress
in cowgirl shirts and jeans, go camping, hike,
and love again—or still—the man I loved so much
at twenty-one. Ahead, a red-tailed hawk planes high,
arcing, hovering on unseen currents, using
contraries, as errors are auxiliaries to being, a necessary
dark side of the mirror, its truth the brighter for it—
light, clear water running, vast reflections. All is well.

6: Pike's Peak, October

The summer was perfection—painted skies,
clouds gathering by four, dark scrolls of rain;
then bursting red that took us by surprise,
projecting sunset to the eastern plain.

And friends from South Dakota, Illinois,
Wyoming, Texas, England came like birds
and perched. We sat *al fresco* to enjoy
the view, good wine, blue cheese, delight in words.

It's now October, and the famous peak
by three is pink with horizontal rays
revealing every texture, form, and streak,
a spotlit masterpiece of shorter days.

Though aspen shine still on the Rampart Range,
light snowfall higher up can give me pause,
while colder nights assault the ash and change
wind-scattered leaves to weak, arthritic claws.

It's not just nature, since *my* autumn's here
already, mellow, though—a ripe caress;
love rediscovered late becomes us, Dear,
refining finish of our lives' finesse.

The mountain's body takes on shadow, blue
and secretive, as by a lover's art.
How wild the clouds that crown the peak, how true!
How wide and full the spaces of the heart!

Shamrock

When you invited me to dine and dance,
you chose the grand Shamrock Hotel, the dream
of Glenn McCarthy, wildcatter supreme.
I did not know it was a lifetime's chance.

The famous setting fit you—eyes clear green,
long Irish upper lip, dark, wavy hair.
With tan, taut muscles, brilliant, debonair,
you were the finest man I'd ever seen.

There, you proposed to me. We drank champagne,
made starry plans, got married in the spring.
We were two swallows sporting on the wing,
two soldered lives, a geminated chain.

We can't remember quite what went so wrong.
Although the slope at first seemed smooth as glass,
we found erosion, cracks, a deep crevasse.
It was my fault: I heard the foolish song

of vanity, was pleased, and lost my head.
You went out to the California coast,
while I, deserting you I loved the most,
imagined that I wanted life instead.

This story is not unfamiliar: few
would be unwilling to emend their past.
For decades, then, I thought the die was cast.
Now, wonderfully, we've begun anew.

→

The Shamrock has been razed, an urban crime;
grave topiary figures guard the ground.
We dance again, though, to a seasoned sound,
love surfacing, affirmed in measured time.

Shadow

These snapshots date from nineteen fifty-five,
on New Year's Day. My mother, never good
with cameras, agreed to try, and stood
to photograph the two of us—alive

with happiness, enamored, young. Her head
and arms in shadow at one corner mar
the shots, an unintended avatar
of forebears wary of the marriage bed.

That image lingered on my very ground
for years. From muting of the body's lyre,
such was the irony of my desire
that strings, though taut, could not release a sound.

The music broke at last, its melody
sweet water running over rocks. Her shade
forgives me, surely, as the past, replayed
in mind so often, is amended: see

what you and I, in love again, allow
each other, marvelously—passion, wit,
and pardon—thereby letting me remit
her words and mine, and love you better now.

Sleeping to Haydn

Regardless of desire, location, hour,
some barely sleep, or have to take a pill;
some sleep to *anything*, and have the power
to fall off like a stone, as if at will.

Dear Pat—he's frequently insomniac,
composes and does math while he's abed,
or rouses from his sleep and can't get back—
but here, to compensate, has drooped his head.

According to our new domestic rite,
we set our evenings in a happy key:
good dinner, wine, and music. For tonight,
Chopin ballades, a Haydn symphony.

He's nodded off to Haydn's pure conceit,
as drowsy students close their eyes in class.
The movement lulls him by its rhythmed feat—
cantabile in strings and sonorous brass.

His breathing's even, and he looks serene:
as music's said to soothe the savage breast,
it charms his Irish spirit, a poteen
evoking secret visions, unexpressed.

There's no surprise: he will not stir until
he's shaken, or the measured phrases cease.
Here come crescendos, horns and drums, a trill,
a chord, another chord, a last release.

The silence wakens him; he rolls his eyes,
looks sheepish, smiles, dispensing dreams. Conjoint,
agreeing that the concert's done, we rise,
and wordlessly embrace in counterpoint.

Éventail

—In homage to Stéphane Mallarmé

i

Though Occidental to my fingernails,
how can I not admire Asian art?—
A vase of cloisonné, two Indian veils,
an oval tray, in red (my lacquered heart);

a Burmese Buddha by a Chinese screen
with lilies, hanging boughs, and water fowl;
a gold-veined serving plate of apple green,
a box for cigarettes, a nacred bowl;

a '30s child's kimono from Japan,
six coffee spoons of different designs;
and this, my favorite, a painted fan
of heavy pleated silk, with ivory spines—

these objects, of inheritance or choice,
most nonchalantly scattered on a shelf,
afford my fantasies an Eastern voice,
illuminating difference in myself.

ii

Now, when I spread the fan of peacock hue
and feel the ripple of its artful breeze,
imagining the whistling of bamboo
or blossoms rustling on the cherry trees,

an *éventail* of Stéphane Mallarmé,
composed for Méry, also beats the air
—the ultimate French poet of his day,
whose preciosities beyond compare

embroidered finely on exquisite themes,
like miniatures of the Orient;
and from a fan, a kiss, and fragile dreams
devised in verse a lasting ornament—

as by the aura folded in the pleats
of latent wing that complements a glove,
arise such immaterial conceits,
the aromatic essence of a love.

"The Trout"

We're listening this evening to "The Trout"—
piano, strings, bright chords and melody,
five voices sounding, moving in and out
in stichomythia, as if for me,

for you. Such fluent lines that have endured
past Schubert's death, in pure, harmonic scheme,
configure how love's music should be heard,
imaginatively, alike as dream

and shade materialized. At play between
technique, thus, and the realm of the ideal,
the notes splash lucidly, a course foreseen,
yet free. Beyond the rapids, we can feel

the current easing, coolly nonchalant,
though carrying still the taut intent of art—
as by concatenation and detente
love's late commotion settles in my heart.

To Former Students, Who Would Be Skeptical

Get ready, students, for today's surprise,
such that you barely would believe your eyes,
were you to see me now. I'm not the same,
except (just temporarily) my name.
Not that I'd cancel quizzes, change the Gide
assignment, skip tutorials you need,
nor let you miss your weekly dose of Proust.
Instead, old chickens have come home to roost,

and I'm distracted, dreamy, quite unfit
to play my role as you'll remember it.
So can you guess? "Good gracious, heavens above—
but yes ... our old professor is in love!"
"A teenager" is what my daughter said,
observing that I seemed out of my head,
till I explained my giddiness. "Why, Mom,
I'd think you'd made a fortune in dot.com,

or got the Nobel Prize, or won a cruise
around the world for two. What stunning news!"
Severe, I was, of yore, quite formal, firm—
not cruel, but known for making students squirm
when questioned on the pleonastic *ne*,
subjunctive tenses, adjectival *le*.
I kept strict time; and if a student dared
to come in late, I paused a moment, glared,

→

resumed, and let him shuffle to his seat,
while others looked away or scraped their feet.
They must have thought I was a metronome,
French poetry and prose my only home,
hard notably in matters of the heart:
"You love a girl; so what? The class must start!"
Unbending as to trysting out of town
when tests were scheduled, I was seen to frown,

then wryly smile, explaining with a cough
it wasn't advantageous to take off.
The wheel of fortune turns: so in my case,
I'm now approximately in your place,
besotted, while you carry on careers.
Strange mollifying in my later years!
Consider then this comment by a sage:
To fall in love is good at any age.

Watermarks

i

In nineteen fifty-eight or thereabout
(it was a matter of a date and name),
we took an Irishman to dinner, out
at San Jacinto Inn; was he the same

great Seamus Heaney, as you thought (his fame
enhanced now by a Nobel Prize)? In doubt,
you wrote to ask me. When your email came,
amazed, incredulous, I gave a shout,

and nearly levitated from my chair.
It's not the poet who excited me, but you.
Some forty years had passed; abruptly, there

in electronic form, as if alive,
the proof that you remembered me—that true,
though distant, love might still survive.

ii

The oysters had faint tastes of gasoline,
as Heaney noted (didn't you agree?).
How strange, reliving time, the feeling keen,
yet foreign. As an inlet draws the sea,

your message, and the next, across the screen,
attracted deep, confluent waves in me,
eliciting a sentimental lien
abeyant, gathering the heart's debris

→

and bits of flotsam from the decades spent
apart. A year's gone by; beside the bay,
where currents swirl in their accomplishment,

we feast on oysters, poems, wine, with sparks
of wit, and watch outrigger lights at play,
bright hieroglyphics, high love's watermarks.

The Anvil

It's June. Above Pike's Peak, which evening drapes
with shade, hammer and anvil form in clouds
afire, beating out fantastic shapes,
flame-red, green, gold, which change to smoky shrouds,

as we must turn to shadow. Still, the night
leaves generous margins, serendipitous,
like our remarriage—late adventure, light
prolonged. It's pure romance, with ease—no fuss,

malentendu, mistrust. A fairy tale
in fact, except for needles of regret,
since, foolish, we allowed ourselves to fail
and missed each other's life. We won't forget,

though, all that kismet granted us—its chance
collateral—while keeping us apart:
a woman at loose ends, met on a ranch;
my darling daughter, given from the heart.

The anvil's dim, the hammer disappears;
but love's forged, lastingly, a diamond chain—
accomplished constellation of long years,
its dazzling suns drawn in by Fate's dark seine.

Bougainvillea: An Epithalamium

—For P.S.

True love is flaming, like geranium,
red roses, poppies, scarlet gilia,
impatiens, crimson-red chrysanthemum,
bright Indian paintbrush, bougainvillea.

Along the panes of our solarium,
which by the water makes a bloomy spa,
you'll find a purple Oriental plum,
whose blossoms—tissue-paper bells—peal "Ah!";

up higher still, a stately Austral gum
that honors dryads' arborphilia;
and, through low vines, the moderated hum
of honey bees plying an aria.

This garden, with its pool and leisured thrum
of soughing winds at home, is really a
heart's paradise, for that's where we've become
one life, beneath the bougainvillea.

II

The Sparrow

—In memory of F. K. H.

Until the final months I didn't see she'd aged much—
always a lively little sparrow, flying, flitting about,
singing, whistling like a bird, planting crocuses
in March, cultivating summer roses, entertaining
friends, generous and giving joy, loving all those
who loved her, sometimes others. Born in 1900,
not robust, ever, she'd had rheumatic fever, spent
seven years abed—survived, endured; she studied

chemistry and read prodigiously, played the organ,
and loved an Irishman (I think) but never married,
perhaps because her elder sister, although comely,
had not wed; or had my grandfather discouraged
suitors? It was another world, then. Aunt Flora
worked, however —Grandfather permitted that—
cared devotedly for aged parents, was a companion
for her sister—two old women, not well matched,

but having no one else. In 1968 she nearly died—
lymphoma. Later, with my daughter, just a girl,
we traveled. No one laughed so, or loved beauty
more. We'd order ouzo or old-fashioneds; in Dijon,
under the cathedral wings, she discovered kir. She'd
hang spoons from her nose in restaurants, converse
with patrons, tell jokes to the waiters: one nearly fell
across the table, fascinated with her; and a famous

→

author found himself in love. We watched the seals
from shipboard in the Inland Passage, took a tour
along the Yukon, visited the Russian church at Sitka;
she bloomed, a tundra flower. In Martinique we rode
by taxi on precarious shelf roads in the volcanic hills,
lunched well, browsed in shops, bought local trinkets
and perfume from Paris. It gave to her the heady feel
of youth, a jewel half-missed, reinvented, valued

in old age, but veined with melancholy—sunlight
falling aslant, dazzling, on the dark sea to the west,
a Wedgwood bowl with ripened pears, a mellow
horn sounding farewell through woods of memory.
She died the winter afterwards. Ah, Aunt Flora!
Re-reading after thirty, forty years these letters
that I wrote—your gift from the grave—I'm ready
to begin again, the phrases taking form in my mind:

I too am growing old; I need your love and counsel,
and wish to give you mine. Can one converse, then,
with the dead? I'd like to let you know of my new
happiness—you who were my harbor in the old seas
of misery—and say that I'm again beside the man
you wanted for me and who loved you greatly also—
that, eliciting your presence, we perceive your voice
in ours, see by your bright eyes, affirm you in us both.

Louise at the Piano

By four o'clock, the housework done, she boils the water
for her tea, takes off her apron, sits a moment
with her cup in hand, sipping, musing. Then it's time
for the piano, hands well washed, keys dusted off
again, as every day—a ritual. A bit of Czerny

and of Bach, for warming up, and then it's Beethoven,
the "Pathétique," the "Tempest." She remembers
Fontainebleau that summer—thirty-nine—and Boulanger,
Casadesus, the other students, riveted to music,
while the war, collecting *leitmotivs*—the Rhineland,

Austria, and Munich, sounds from Spain, a Soviet march—
composed its opening bars, to come with cymbals
in September; then its winter themes in *sostenato*
and the crashing chords through the Ardennes
in May. Her brother died during that war, another body

charred; her parents, stricken, lived to mourn, then let
their grief consume them. Now, Louise herself
is old, with Fontainebleau gone quickly as a dream,
performing done. Her knuckles have become arthritic
knobs; her wrists are swollen from tuberculosis

of the bone—or is it constant housework, an obsessive
search after perfection, a surrogate for love? Still,
she plays, each afternoon, in solitude. She shaped herself
to be an artist, gave up friends, sought the ideal.
Alas. Well, better loneliness than other things, she says.

→

Yet, were it possible, would she trade her brilliant tone
and mastery, her concert tours, for the experience
of the heart she never had, romance, the risks
of suffering—her trust betrayed, or marriage without
love, ungrateful children, loss? No happiness is whole,

and genius must be purchased by some sacrifice.
Wistfully, Louise spoke once about a man named Charles,
a suitor long ago. What happened was not said;
but surely he desired her, proposed, perhaps; and she,
uncertain or afraid, or driven to be alone, denied

him. All of that is dust—illusions, lovely flesh, bright
innocence; she's worn, without fulfilment or the ripeness
of a woman given to another, at least once. The music
radiates—its passion, light at sunset, coral, gold,
and rose harmonics, layered over dark clouds of distress.

Lieutenant Fran

—In memory of E.B.M.

Francesca was her name, unusual
where she grew up—the peaks of the Front Range
and westward, highland pastures, little towns:
Red Cliff and Carbondale, then Woodland Park.
She was a ranger's daughter, weaned on snow,
iron stoves, wild blazes, kerosene, hard work,
and horses. Thus her world was circumscribed:
vast outlook, narrow compass. She went down

to study nursing—surgery. The war
reached to America; she volunteered,
the way you'd fight a fire on the Peak.
Lieutenant Fran, they called her. In the wards,
she met an aviator, Donald, there
to see a friend. Their love was brief, perfumed
by antiseptic. Donald then flew back
to Burma and rejoined the remnant band

called Flying Tigers, fighting still. She too
shipped out, and felt her stomach heave, unused
to water, but she got to England, worked
in hospitals, and waited for the V-
mails Donald sent—soft insects bearing flame,
sweet birds. In June of '44 she crossed to France
and landed from a Higgins boat. Behind
the lines, four miles or so, large tents were pitched

→

to treat the wounded; there, Fran worked amid
the strafings, bombs, disorder, pain, and death—
an image of the war. They moved inland
through the *bocage* of Normandy, a maze
composed of woods and hedges. Later came
the Bulge. Once, Patton visited, and bulled
his way around the tent. Red Crosses meant
so little—they, it seemed, attracted fire,

blood drawing down the sanguinary flames.
Francesca took without complaint the cold,
the dying men; she thought of Donald, far
away in China or the Hump, and felt
each day, with luck or not, was good, because
it meant another chance for war to end,
and both of them to live. Her parents knew,
though barely, of her fiancé; he had

his people in Nevada. Somehow, news
went round: he had been killed. Her father wrote,
with facts, but feeling. When she opened it,
the letter burned its lines into her hands,
then in her memory. She persevered,
endured, imagining each wounded man
she treated as the one she loved—past hope,
but in her heart alive still, needing her,

because she needed him; and when men died,
despite her care, she grieved the more. In Rheims
on V-E Day, she saw the ancient seat
of kings and Christendom aglow with light
unseen for years—both flames of victory
and light funereal. She stayed in France
till forty-six. Back stateside finally,
discharged, she nursed a diabetic man,

old, rich, and then chauffeured his widow—friend,
resource, companion—through the countryside
until she died in turn. We live on death,
a dialectic old as love and war,
and on fortuitous connections, chance
encounters: someone present in the wake
of loss, a piece of driftwood one can seize,
the dangling line of hope. Francesca met

a good man in the Springs, divorced, alone.
Four children—evidence of love and fate's
imponderable ways—were born.—What then
do we owe destiny? We are its wheat
and chaff, its tracks and random leavings. Fran
remarked that life had dealt a decent hand;
instead, she was its strange accomplishment,
a star ablaze amidst expanding dust.

Fire in the Mind

—In memory of M. A. C. P.

Among a stack of old spring binders filled
with notes—the trophies, or the detritus,
of forty years of teaching, taken home
like ashes from a crematorium—
this jewel, not mine: a senior thesis, bound,
from nineteen sixty-two, done by a girl
who'd learned sufficient French in just four years
to write so well, with such authority,

that, as I leaf through now, I am amazed.
She wrote on Simone de Beauvoir. Our minds
met easily, and in her prose my hand
is sometimes visible—the mentor's genes.
She also was a darling of her class,
the Queen of Rondelet, a "Beauty," rich
in flair, charm, wit. She even cooked. Two men
who both became Rhodes Scholars courted her,

but they went off to Oxford, while she took
her doctorate in history, then left
for Paris, favored *haute couture*, and did
translation. Once we lunched al fresco, near
the Louvre—friends still, in the prime of life—
but spoke of trivial things. She later wed
in his château a wealthy Frenchman, not
an intellectual, and smoked herself

to death. She's buried in the family vault
in Père-Lachaise. A close friend tried to find
the grave, but wandered vainly in that maze,
a honeycomb, until she heard a voice
instructing her to leave: "Go buy yourself
a bottle of expensive French perfume,
in memory of me." —Forever gone,
long evenings spading in the library,

the thrilling mastery of that new tongue,
the hunt for ignis fatuus, happiness,
elusive always; gone that perfect sphere
of consciousness, a bubble, full—delight
and disaffection, laughter, cough. What I
inherit are these words in carbon black,
as on a cavern wall, the signs that speak
of winged illusions, fire in the mind.

Envoi

Dear Mary Ann, your old professor says:
Work diligently there in Père-Lachaise.
You see things better from the other shore,
as mortal matters give concern no more.
You can't be interrupted in the tomb
when studying the cryptic book of doom;
distractions must be few, and time permits
the leisured application of your wits.
You'll reach a new perfection in your style,
observe the human comedy the while,
and see things pass that we cannot yet see,
the very spirit of all history.

Carnations

—In memory of E. P. P.

Carnations in a bowl, deep red, with fern
and baby's breath, adorn the summer day,
their ruching gathered at the sepals' urn
like flounces on a bodice. In the play

of eyes, they flutter, moths along the wall,
or, smouldering, revive in crystal flame;
and leaves inclined to shadow curl and fall
as casually as tears without a name,

while tender motions waver in the heart,
then modulate into a minor key,
devising darkly by consummate art
bouquets of radiance and green debris.

Carafes

—Musée d'Art Moderne, Paris

The grayish ground of canvasses, the wall, room, garden
glimpsed in gauze—all surrounding space devolves
upon these painted objects by Morandi, dense in being,
emptying out the rest. Mere earthenware, they are,
or glass, pale yellow, creamy, ochre, vaguely green or blue:
small bowls and slender bottles and carafes, repeated

coolly through the room, contested selves embraced
in difference and identity. They hold me, but hold nothing
else, entire by themselves. Collected at the center
of the scene, they huddle, as it were, to gain solidity
and presence, lest some nothingness of gaze disturb them.
Clutching at existence, one cannot be too attentive:

past the frames lurk threats of absence and annihilation—
as, beyond the edge, the universe falls off into a vortex,
black and void.—Here, mind and matter meet in stillness;
movement might be threatening. Notice, though,
a sudden rippling of sensation, weightless as a thought
that glances over sunlit water—followed by a hush,

quite palpable, a silencing of motion and of speech,
as if disorder lay below the surface, ready to break out.—
What! Two women stop to chat, aloud, denying
the intensity of paint. One reaches in her handbag, finds
a pen, a small address book, scribbles something. *I*
am not unmoved: it's sacrilege, a *lèse-peinture*; and yet

→

the paintings are untouched, beyond all violation: leather
from Lancel, a Hermès scarf, have lost their power.
Did this carafe look back at me just now, the artist's eye
compacted with his vision in the clay? Charmed, the snake
of being rises, twisted, eyes like carbuncles, as if
to strangle our contingency. Yet feelings somehow lift,

a tone, a texture smoothed: reality has been distilled,
the ponderous presence of the paintings lightening in me,
their objectivity spun out into the very substance
of idea. I can depart, as after incantations, full of finite
things, and watch the clouds amass on canvasses
of Paris skies, the darkness exorcized, the alien serene.

Marmalade

Her husband was a London barrister,
connected to St. James. That is, before
he went to Texas. He played poker, too,
not well, and lost, it seems—or *not*, perhaps,
depending on your view. It's known he played
with some investors who acquired a tract
of Panhandle, the White Deer Lands, along
a creek that cuts the *Llano*, flowing north

to the Canadian. He gambled on,
and drained his assets; but a debt to him
may have been paid in land. In any case,
when Philip William Williams Morgan came
to Texas, what he had, or bought, was just
enough to start a ranch. Elizabeth,
his wife, had packed her dresses, said goodbye
to London, and accompanied him out

to nowhere. That was founders' time; they lived—
like Goodnight, Duncan, Franklin, all—
in struggle with the longhorns, weather, earth.
Their dwelling was a dugout; yet she rode
side-saddle, English-style, and wore long gowns;
remembering England's green and pleasant land,
they planted trees of British species. Still,
it was not home: the harshness, solitude,

→

dry thunderheads, fierce glare, and torrid winds,
then winter freezes. She gave birth, alone,
as if she'd been abandoned, in a storm,
when Philip had gone out while blizzard snows
whirled round, primeval, turbulent. A boon,
the railroad had come through in 'eighty-seven,
connecting her in thought, at least; but floods
and train wrecks proved it vulnerable. Once

in a derailment, though, the boxcars fell,
broke open, spilled their contents. Oranges!
The little globes, like lanterns, lit the range
with color and exotic charm. But since
they would not last, Elizabeth, right then,
decided to make marmalade. Huge vats,
used for the laundry, were brought in and washed;
the other women, bringing sugar, stayed

to learn. What memories bubbled there, what sweet
effusions of the past! And tartness too—
strange melancholy of a life, its zest
and piquancy. She looked out later, watched
the sun descend, a glorious, ripened fruit,
across the *Llano*, caught a honeyed scent
of juice, and felt how valences had changed,
time ripening and paying debts in joy.

Madeleine Gide in Algeria

She was his cousin, loved by him in soul
from childhood; never in the body, though.
And she was older, too—a wounded bird,
who'd found her mother with a lover, seen
her father die of grief. At twenty, Gide
proposed to her, but frightened her instead.
He persevered; his mother disapproved,
with aunts and uncles. So he temporized,

pursued his literary life, "self-launched,"
wrote strange, revealing books, then with a friend
sailed for North Africa. It was a true
beginning for him, though he first fell ill—
bad blood coughed nightly into handkerchiefs,
febrilic days. When he emerged at last
by metamorphosis, it was rebirth—
a new-come Adam and New Covenant,

if quite unorthodox. Some Arab boys
invited him to an oasis—sun,
fresh, quickening water, breezes, palms.
His senses now awakened, he rebelled
against his puritan's morality.
A strange child in the sand dunes offered him
his body; Gide unfolded his desire
in consummation. Then, with Oscar Wilde,

→

he met Mohammed, a musician boy.
When Gide proposed to buy some property,
or take an Arab youth with him to France,
his family, shocked, assumed he was deranged.
Fate intervened: Gide's mother, dying, changed
her mind about the marriage, convinced
no doubt that only Madeleine might save
him from himself. His uncle Charles agreed;

they married, thus, half-blind and half-aware,
Gide anchoring her, fatherless, forlorn,
and she, the mystic mother substitute.
Like many other unions, theirs was smooth
along the surface, turbulent below,
and founded on misunderstanding, churned
to anguish. They set out for Switzerland,
cold home of Protestants, then Italy,

Tunisia, and Algeria, the lands
of André's longing. He was restless; she
said nothing, and endured. At night he fled
their rooms, went prowling to renew himself
by furtive contacts, faces in a crowd,
men's baths. He watched Mohammed making love
with "Daniel B." and was repulsed, but still,
by *clair-obscur* of sensuality

and lust within a lucid mind, pursued
his brown-skinned boys. *She* was restraint,
impediment; *he*, vagabond desire.
Yet she remained the lifeline of his world,
the prop of genius, mediator, ground.
The torture lasted more than forty years.
Though ill, she left with him for Africa
once more, in ninety-nine. They took a train

44

departing from El Kantara. Three lads,
half-naked, in the next compartment leaned
their torsos through the window; Gide reached out
and stroked their amber flesh, his breathing hard.
"You seemed a lunatic, a criminal,"
she told him later, all illusions gone.
She knew it meant a sentencing—her shame,
her shattered love, herself the price of art.

Mina Loy in Mexico

In some ways, she was fortune's favorite—
intelligent, tall, beautiful, endowed
with charm, and talented for poetry
and painting. But such gifts exact a price,
it seems: misfortune and unhappiness.
She'd trained for art in Munich, then returned
to London, studied with Augustus John,
gone next to Paris with a pastor's son,

Haweis, an ugly man, who may have raped
her once. They married nonetheless—an act
of protest or escape. In France, they moved
among expatriates—knew Gertrude Stein,
Brancusi, Futurists. She showed her work
in the salons—dark pencil or gouache,
slim female figures, almost mannerist—
and changed her name from Lowy, in '04,

to hide her Jewishness, or show dislike
of parents and constraints, or to suggest
that she would be a *law* unto herself.
She left for Florence next, met Mabel Dodge,
lived giddily in that aesthetic sphere,
loved Marinetti, then Papini, left
Haweis, abandoning her children, too.
She traveled to New York, and followed all

its eddying currents—drama, politics,
and painting—meeting some of Mabel's crowd
again, utopians, Wobblies, Socialists.
Then Arthur Cravan, really Fabian Lloyd,
a cosmopolitan of six-feet-four
whose aunt had married Oscar Wilde, became
her lover. He had been a Dadaist
in France. A pugilist and writer too,

he'd won respect for vanguard poetry
and brawls; he'd lasted several rounds, it's said,
against Jack Johnson. He had documents,
but mostly forged; in wartime, Mexico
under Carranza sounded promising—
a land where such irregulars as he
could flourish, with deserters, rustlers, thieves
and Pancho Villa, "Gertrude Stein as man,"

in Mabel's words. Divorced now, Mina took
a train, alone, got past the border, reached
the capital, where Arthur had arrived
before her. Politics were fiery—
Red Russians, Indian rebels, Japanese—
but she was poor, and cold. The two survived
on boxing matches, stratagems, and friends.
She wanted to get married, to offset

her early, loveless choice; and they adored
each other. Hurdles fell, after a farce
or two. The Mexicans, now reconciled
with Washington, were keen on seeking out
deserters from all armies; Cravan knew
he might be caught, shipped to New York, and sent
to prison or to war. They hid and ran,
and nearly starved; and Mina was with child.

→

With others, they went down to Veracruz
to sail for Buenos Aires; but police
were searching vessels there. They met again
on the Pacific, in Salina Cruz.
With money from his boxing, Arthur bought
a leaky boat. He stroked it like a girl
and patched it; Mina cooked, and mended sails,
and watched him work. Impatient, he took off

for Puerto Ángel, to the west; he'd trade
the craft for something larger, and they'd leave
for Chile. Mina stood, her stomach ripe,
and gestured wildly as he tacked and turned,
and disappeared onto the lustrous mirror
of sea. It was forever. Mina hoped—
a torch—and waited on the beach for days,
till her companions wrested her away and sent

her on a ship to South America.
She later searched for him, obsessively.
There were reports and sightings—all mirage,
or flashes of marsh fire. At night, she dreamt
him into being, catching words in winds
that carried him; she saw him fly, an erne,
above the sea, or rising from the troughs
and coming toward her, bloody sails for hands.

Desire

The look is dark, not golden—eyebrows tight,
a glassy concentration in the eyes,
the pupils narrowed, and the candid light
of irises assuming a disguise,

as if one were a stranger in desire,
possessed by, to possess, another mind,
the primal urge of wild men by the fire,
of animals demented by their kind.

There are no wasted motions; all is grave,
imperative, the words as dense as stone;
and pleasure turns immortal in the cave
where absolute *to be* resides with bone.

He bends to show his mastery, and shame
with her consent the body wholly bared,
submitted to a will she cannot name,
which violates her own but must be shared.

Withdrawing to himself, he hears the sense
of being magnified in heavy breath,
with knowledge, consciousness of knowledge, thence
in mirrored destiny to knowing death.

D. H. Lawrence in the Hopi Lands

"Who is that Mormon over there,
emaciated, with the putty face
and reddish whiskers, pale?" The question, put
by Laura Armer—painter, writer too—
was reasonable, since the fellow had
black, flat-topped headgear of the sort preferred
by Mormons then and sold at trading posts.
The answer, though, was unexpected; "That

is D. H. Lawrence." They had driven long—
some thousand miles, in all—from Taos, he
and Frieda, Tony, Mabel, to observe
the Hopi Snake Dance, on Third Mesa top
at Hotevilla, then ride on to view
Canyon de Chelly. He had been skeptical,
disdainful of the Indians, the brown
and primitive, who made him yearn again

for Europe; he loathed tourists. Still, he sat,
with others, on the ground, by Armer's feet,
to watch the rite as desert holy men
held rattlesnakes—becalmed somehow, well-washed
and oiled, but writhing hard—between their teeth.
The corn dance in New Mexico was strange,
yet subtle—like the Zuni rituals,
neat, beautiful; the Hopis' was grotesque,

though mystical—a marriage of the good
and evil, recognizing poison's power,
intended to domesticate the will
of darkest spirits and appropriate
their potency. Lorenzo likewise wished
to find the hidden Source, not God
but gods, and yield to their beneficence;
thus he who preached to women dominance

by men was mastered as the Hopis whirled,
responding to the horns of darkness, fear,
malevolence and venom, challenging
themselves, the world. The vipers sometimes fell
and slithered off, but were pursued and caught
with sticks, and dancers took them in their mouths
again; while Lawrence, mesmerized, advanced
just slightly, thinking of the bright green snake

he'd painted on the door of Mabel's house,
entwined around a sunflower—potent signs
of heavens, earth, desire. The dancers' limbs
and serpents radiated—arrows shot
at life, with sapience and courage sharp
enough to pierce its core. Lorenzo let
vitality flow through him—heroes' strength—
but wore his lungs out in the cosmic song.

Such Quiet Now

—For L. H. F.

i

Such quiet, now that afternoon
is emptied of its cymbal clouds
and its horn of rain—except for
the thought that will not leave,
like a grieving woman's dream,
that death must be remembered.

ii

The tree frogs now are whirring
in the cedars, and the wind
is roused; a bird slants off
into the sun. Even at dusk, I
cannot stare down the heavens.
I would say to you if I could,
"Lynn, it is not your loneliness
that distresses me most for you
tonight, but the resistance
of the hard sky as you look up."

iii

I remember the time you cried
after class over St.-John Perse,
and how I did not know whether
it was difficulties of the Antillean
verse, or its taut loveliness.
Thinking how you face this death,

such emotion makes me afraid,
the burden of contentment quite
enough for you, and now also
the bitter berries of your grief.

iv

A faintest wake of light still
divides the sky; then the white
edges roll under into dark. No
answer comes, although the trees
stir as if in sleep, and a tide
of stars dips so low we might wade
in. How fraternal is the world—
yet how strange. The adventure
ends in ruins. I see for you no
window into night, but cast to you
these words, among the luminous
sea markings on a distant field.

Fortune's Choice

—In memory of L. L. M.

Her parents later told her how they'd left
their flat and their possessions, everything,
in minutes, when her father realized
the Nazis would invade. Her mother cried,
"We *can't go!* With new velvet curtains!" Still,
they went—good rats of sinking Belgium, signs
that it was doomed. From Antwerp, they set out
for France, reached Paris, headed for the south,

where farmers sheltered them in the Basses-Alpes.
They lived like beetles, in a carapace,
away from towns and the *Milice.* The hills
were sweet with lavender in forty-three
while *Feldgrau* swarmed, polite but deadly, armed
and making Fortune's random choices. Jeanne
was sent—an innocent at play—to count
the German trucks that passed along the road;

it was an education for the world.
The family reached New Orleans, in the tide
of refugees, and prospered. Jeanne, grown up,
had wit and European polish; scars
from dread and dislocation were concealed
inside. She met the captain of a ship
from Hamburg, twice her age. One rendezvous
sufficed to snare her, wary though she was—

love holds its prisoners by spell: blue eyes,
a voice you can't forget, a certain stride
or smile. Her parents learned of the affair
and made her break if off. That didn't last.
Despite her promise, when he next returned
she waited for him in a hotel bar.
Her father, there on business, happened by;
she glimpsed him in the mirror, quickly turned,

looked down. One evening, though, the lovers stopped
for traffic on the toll bridge; in the lane
adjacent were her parents' closest friends.
Her father's anguish sounded a new note—
not loathing of his enemies, but love
deceived. Withdrawing, he let life drain out.
It was the end; she married someone else,
to pay her debt. Or was it that she sensed

(an animal again, a refugee)
the wing of illness over her? The man
was good, as Fate decided. While her mind
watched frantically, her body turned to wood,
her muscles gone, her throat constricted, choked,
her eyelids moving to say yes or no—
the lavender of France fresh by her side,
pain of the past and beauty in one breath.

Translations from the *Rymes* of Pernette du Guillet

To please the one who tortures me, I fain
Would seek no remedy for my torment:
For, seeing he is happy in my pain,
In his contentment I must be content.

****

If serving you deserves a recompense,
And compensation is desire's peace,
I would then serve you always, even more
Than thought, so that my pleasure will not cease.

****

In Dauphiné as Ceres harvested the wheat,
At Millery god Bacchus pressed the purple wine:
Wherefore I can foresee, the juice being so green,
That Venus will be frosty in the wintertime.

****

It was for me so very dark a night
That it obscured both Heaven and Earth, a ban
So great that even at noon I could not see
A shape or likeness, sorely grieving me:
But when at last I saw the dawn appear—
A thousand colors, various and clear—
I was so full of joy at seeing light
Around me, everywhere, that I began
To praise aloud the one whose love unfurled
This sash of brilliant Daylight in the World.

****

This great renown of your commanding art
And learning shows you have a generous part
Of each exquisite grace; yours is the true
Enjoyment of the gifts of Heaven. Few
Can know that nonetheless you bring great care
Into my mind, which lacks the promptitude
To thank the Heavens for the time I share
With him, in whom the Graces, captured there,
Are yet content with such a servitude
Through all the good with which he is endued!

****

Since it has pleased you that I should be known,
And by your hand, this VICE TO BE TRANSFORMED,
I shall attempt to make this goodness grow
In me, which can alone change me to you:
It is by knowing how much I shall strive
That you will recognize that by the same
Intent I flee the vice of ignorance,
Since you desire to change me as from black
To white, and by this service high arrange
That in my error THIS VICE YOU WILL CHANGE.

****

By these ten lines I must myself accuse
Of not quite knowing how to honor you,
Except in wishing so, a weak excuse:
But how can one adorn in writing one
Who all alone can make himself adored?
I do not say that if I had your skill
I would not then acquit myself at will,
At least of all the good that you assure

→

In me. Then lend me eloquence, and see
How I will praise you well, as you praise me!

****

Alone, subjected to the stanza, R
Has, rightly, put me in the greatest care
Concerning harm that one may have, or good,
By R. For R in error can be understood
As meaning that the compliments which I
Receive are false, or R is nothing, save
Remainder. If one wishes a reply
By R, I say, although I do not have
The skill, nor virtues that your R declares,
That I make err each man whose praise I bear.

****

No longer need I care if day deceive
Me, or there falls a moonless, wintry night;
For all that can do nothing, I believe,
To harm me, since my Day, with softened Light,
Illuminates me wholly, so much more
That in my mind at midnight I perceive
What with my eyes I never saw before.

****

The more I wish, the less an adverse fate
Will grant that I may see the one to whom,
By many a quarrel, she could have done much harm
And torment, if it were not true that he
Possesses from the Heavens this happy bent,
To reach his purpose always. Whence with him
I have the pure, consoling sentiment,
That, he contented, I remain content.

****

My body thrilled, my spirit is amazed
With wonder at the joy that touches me,
Delighting me with love, which wakens all
By this one good, which makes us call it God.
But if you wish to consummate its power,
You must desist in that desire: its dart
Will turn toward it, inflaming it the more,
And love increase in every lover's heart.

III

Burning in Louvain

—August 1914–November 1917

"Where one burns books, there in the end burn men"—
so Heine wrote. Thus Bruno's thought, before
the man himself was burnt, was set ablaze;
the learnèd works of Etienne Dolet,
thrice judged a heretic, twice caught, once charred,
were thrown into the fire; the holy wrath
of Torquemada and his ruffians
consigned both books and readers to the stake—

a cold, fanatical *auto-da-fé*. But more
than that: the wealth of learning in those tracts
went underground; obscurantism ruled;
and *it* was worse. Or so I thought, until
the Germans came. My God! The manuscripts,
the books that turned to ash—five hundred years
of learning, loveliness, devotion, labor, love!
From that, I'd made my life; they burnt my heart

along with parchments. Why? Before the war,
the Germans sent fine scholars here; the land
of Goethe, Schiller, Beethoven is theirs,
or *was*; their universities have been
a lamp for centuries. And what was gained
by shelling books? It was vindictive, not
just tactical: a boy, a patriot,
had shot an officer, and others fell

→

to bullets from the windows; at the rear
the column had been harassed. This was *war*,
however; what could they expect? They killed
three hostages—*bourgmestre*, citizens
of note—tossed bombs into the houses, burnt
magnificent creations of the past
in Gothic architecture, Flemish art,
and then attacked the library. I watched

the conflagration from my flat, the smoke,
the flames ascending as in images
of Armageddon, then the crumbling walls,
the crash, the floors collapsing into one
another, like a dream, the layers crushed,
unreal, together. In the exodus
toward the sea, the common things of life—
pathetic flotsam from the wreckage—bobbed

among the human waves that washed the roads—
old kettles, children's mattresses, a cage
without its bird. By chance I had at home,
entrusted to my care, a manuscript,
illuminated. As I left, I wrapped
it in a cloth, then threw it hastily
into my knapsack with a few old clothes,
some biscuits, cheese, and chocolate, a knife,

a bottle of Bordeaux. Along the route,
debris of incunabula and bits
of vellum drifted in the wind, still warm,
it seemed, their ragged edges curled and grey—
some letters visible withal, dark birds
ignited at the wing-tips, eyes on fire,
or angels weeping in a holocaust.
I had no plan, save exile somewhere—France

or England—still uncertain in the great
debacle. On the way toward Ghent, I found
by Providence a small iron chest, cast off
and empty, in a field. The woods nearby
were solitary: in the night I dug
a hole by scratching, dog-like, at the soil
and hacking roots. It was an offering
to past, and future, time. As if my work

had been fulfilled that night, I'll not survive,
I think, this awful war—too old, too ill.
Indeed, it may not end, but drag itself
from Ypres and Verdun to Passchendaele,
devouring everything, toward God knows what
unthinkable catastrophe, until
the last of Europe's blood and mind are gone,
as men decay, dissolve, or burn with books

they would not honor. My impulsive act,
the scribe's long labor—all seems useless now
amid the ruins. I cannot retrieve
the manuscript; the very woods may be
consumed and greater clouds of evil choke
the world, from thought turned diabolical,
as madmen light a pyre of words and flesh,
and set the stream of charity on fire.

Flying Straight

—Brooks Air Force Base, The Early 1970s

i

Returning, stretched out on my back, straight through
from Tokyo to San Antonio,
to home—a country that I loved, and died
for, nearly, but is festering around
our war, as if *we* had decided it . . .—
and still in Texas, convalescing now,
I live it all again—the awful months
of fear, the final firefight, the blood,
then being bound delirious in that plane,
its engines bellowing, the tons of fuel
below me, ready to explode—like swamps
along the Sabine River in a storm,
when flickers of St. Elmo's fire ignite
the pools of darkness with their cypress dance.
One moment, waking feverish, I saw
the empty bunk beside my own, and thought
that Jack Van Horn, a pal, had disappeared
forever, lost back in Japan, or thrown
into the maelstrom of the clouds—until
the vision shattered in a wave of pain.
A spark can set my memory ablaze:
today a girl appeared around the ward
who said she was a friend of Jack Van Horn,
a fellow down the hall. At first, my mind
was pinned by disbelief—as though the name
were still a prisoner of those images;
and yet I see they must have been a dream,
since now the nurse has wheeled that very man

beside my bed—a buddy salvaged from
the night, and 'Nam, and from delirium.
But with the certainty of living flesh,
the questionings besiege my bed again,
as if I were myself a field of fire.

ii

Perhaps the fifties were the last good years.
What's certain is that we are troubled men,
and what we fought for will be lost. Thank God
the ones I cared for most were spared the sight;
but I have seen it for them. Whether those
denouncing us can understand I doubt.
The war was our inheritance: for all
the rhetoric and guilt, I do not know
how history's bloody players could refuse
the roles they were assigned. In any case
I honor, Father, what I can: you fought
your war and I fought mine, and you returned
a hero; and if you believed your war
was clean and just, so much the better. Yet
it all is slaughter, and the dead are dead.
Perhaps, at best, what's worse than war—the camps,
a homeland bombed—could justify what we
have done. The healing will be slow, like wounds
where sutures darken as they reconcile
the ruptured flesh. Outside, the horn of spring
is pouring color out—forsythia
in classic gold, and plumes of scarlet quince;
the companies of bluebonnets and phlox
are dressed in full estate. One always starts
again, each moment, carrying a past
of threads that dangle, or can be undone
and woven for another time and place,

→

another self. I sometimes dream that I
am flying, not indentured to a board
but free, my body like a bird's spread out
in space, and all the spinning world
before me. So it should be when the warriors all
come home, the heroes' bodies dragged no more.

After the Catch

—Spring 1975

Scales alive in the spraying sun,
the gill nets leapt under their load,
before the air-drowned salmon fell
back, strangling in a flood of wind
over the deck; and the boats circled

back dockside, while the struggling
of the fish quieted, iced down to be
bound to our bodies and our strange
events. Who shall say who survives?
Last night, I could not help but think

of the lean shoulders of young men
pulling in their seines, as the lines
of helicopters cast from the carriers
lifted their catch above the Saigon
palaces, while hands were hammered

down the walls, and the refugees
paddled in their sampans, streaming
like spawn. The labyrinthine traps
are full: they have caught the dead,
the legless boys, and now the swarms

of the defeated. I saw the choppers
rise and flit across the screen:
tell me where the stream runs clear,
where the salmon can swim in peace,
beyond the reaches of a dubious law.

Vaux-le-Vicomte

This vast estate, a parvenu's grand dream,
was purchased with the veins of revenue
that Fouquet syphoned by a clever scheme
from royal taxes, as his royal due.

Le Nôtre's gardens, noble in design,
prolonged the classic forms of the château,
whose three pavilions, dome, and rooftop line
proclaimed abroad the genius of Le Vau.

The treasurer loved show and valued wit,
supported Molière and La Fontaine,
and offered lavish entertainments, fit
to magnify the monarch and his reign.

King Louis, though, took umbrage, feeling he
had been humiliated and outdone;
what business has a planet to decree
such grandeur as is only for the Sun?

Fouquet was seized and jailed, and later tried,
charged with corruption and *lèse-majesté,*
condemned to life in prison, where he died,
by Louis, ever jealous of his sway.

How well the house still wears Fouquet's desire!
It's ours, for a few euros and a while:
we wander through, examine things, admire—
late heirs of his cupidity and style;

then pay to see the cupola and bend
to make our way through cobwebs, beams, stale air;
next, take the spiral staircase and ascend
into the "lantern," gaze at the parterre,

and think of Fouquet planning out his climb,
as master *régisseur,* but lucre's slave—
old Fortune's moral for a dazzling time—
now playing to the dark house of the grave.

Saint-Séverin, I

—Left Bank, Paris

To pass the time, and get another caffeine fix
before the beadle opens up Saint-Séverin,
right at eleven, we sit down on a café terrace, just
across, and order our *express*. Except for bustle
at the doors of tiny restaurants—unloading vegetables,
rinsing down the sidewalks, putting out the chairs
and pocket-sized iron tables—it is very quiet
here, with tourists still in bed, or having coffee

and croissants in their hotel, and not yet ready
for another day of obligations. The only other clients
at this hour are from the neighborhood,
most, I think, *habitués*, one slightly drunk already.
The church is buttressed in my memory: *porche*,
nave, rose window, late Gothic spires (hooking clouds
today)—and the cloister, where ten years ago
we drank champagne; and at the prow, breaching

waves of the old town, the apse—rebuilt from rubble
after explosives sheared it off, sparing the rest,
in nineteen-forty-four: low vaulting, mellow
stone, glass of garnet and Aegean blue, a copse
of tracery and branching pillars, and the spiraled lines
of the famous twisted column at the center,
—a sinewy torso by Michelangelo, or a woman
in a swirling gown, cut along the bias, arms lifted,

dancing for the Lord. That May morning, fugue,
toccata, and chorale by Bach leafed out, with sprays
of bridal white and, niched into the great trees
of the nave, greenery like resurrection vine. Tourists
lingered, stared a bit—I heard some whispers
at the side—then ambled on, as the officiant read
the vows, and you two repeated them. Visitors
this time, we'll walk there now, recalling Cana's wine

and benediction, gracious gifts from One who made
life more abundant, whose long torture—nailed
to a denatured tree, his body writhing in great pain—
caused earth to quake, split rocks, extinguished
day, and rent the veil of the old covenant,
until an angel pointed to the bare sarcophagus,
and light restored the world—stone, wood, and bodies
reconciled and whole, all holding heaven's word.

Saint-Séverin, II

With Notre-Dame, the Sacré-Coeur, and all
the rest, obscure or famous—Trinity,
Saint-Julian-the-Poor, Saint-Roch, Saint-Paul—
it's just another Paris church to see.

For we have come too late, I think—the call
to holiness will miss this century;
in recent years there's been another Fall,
with gilded fruit of power on the tree.

But tourists go in anyhow, and weave
wide-eyed through narthex, chapels, transepts, apse
and look as though they wished they could believe,

acknowledging the truth of human lapse
by what proclaims it visibly, alone:
the weightlessness of ransom wrought in stone.

Christ Pantokrator

His right hand raised, its slender fingers curled,
the left hand holding up the holy book,
He offers His salvation to the world
and blessing from the One whom it forsook.

The figure dominates the apse, its cloak
of blue half-open, seeming to embrace
all those who would assume His gentle yoke,
and find redemption in His sacred face.

Reflections from the dome illuminate
with gold the nimbused cross around His head;
below, archangels, Virgin, saints await
the resurrection of the ransomed dead.

His steady eyes appear to turn their gaze
on every viewer—deep, unblinking, dark,
yet luminous and searching as the rays
that light the nave, the covenant's new ark.

Anonymous, just strangers in a crowd,
like those who stood on a Judean hill
to watch, and heard Him as He cried aloud,
we know the power of His passion still:

the letters come alive, the voice is clear,
as though, through two millennia, we heard
the Christ Pantokrator among us here
proclaim, in words, Himself, the perfect Word.

→

What of this wonder can I take away—
with photos, and a very human pride?
The palm of life, a soul become the prey
of burning love, the body glorified.

Birds in the Bush

—just common sparrows, back-lit by the setting sun,
their feathers sharply outlined and their dusky colors
painted in rich oils. Brilliant, too, their chattering—
quick, golden notes of sound, in random sequences
(it seems), aleatory, yet more pleasing than a piece
of toneless modern music. They have gathered here
at cocktail time, below a parasol of greenery, a bush
well trimmed and hollowed out—a bower drawing

them, as we are drawn to margaritas, chips, and salsa,
at this outdoor café. Ceaselessly, they flutter, diving,
flushing up, posing briefly on the branches, scattering
again, performing entrechats, then changing perches
as in musical chairs. Below, the mulchy earth must be
a smorgasbord of seeds; but bits of crisp tortilla, not
disdained, and sandwich crumbs attract the sparrows
to the terrace flagstones, underfoot, and then the table;

here, emboldened, one approaches to investigate a dish,
alighting on its very rim, and looking at me quizzically
as if to ask *permesso.* I could have a bird in hand now,
sure delight for me, sure palpitating of an avian heart;
but do I want to trifle with its little life, the way a king,
holding the living creature, doomed it (in the tale) by
fatal logic, playing god? Ah no: the birds belong there,
fearless, in the bush, which canopies their ideal being

→

as the heavens' tabernacle arches, holding for us gold
of cloud and monstrance sun, glorious against the blue.
The bird pecks briskly at the scraps beside him—little
pearls—and then flies off, brief wingèd gift, brief song.
I watch the sparrows cluster, calmer now, communal,
offering their part of the evening peace. I'll stay here
in contingency, lifting a glass to human imperfection,
as God unseen walks in the garden still, scattering grace.

Butterflies All of One Dark

Bucking a headwind, they ride high,
all of one dark against a harebell blue.
What vigor came by metamorphosis!
So they fly south, on summer's wake,

to flee the cold already closing down.
Winged archipelago! Here, the river
shimmers with a lure of silver light,
as little bodies work above and move

their being in the sun. If I cast my line
to catch their purpose, hold that beat,
could I borrow an eye on heaven, hear
the fugue of time? They run the rapids

of the pine tops, knowing neither me,
nor omens pressed in trampled leaves
—and pass, last passion of the larvae,
arrayed in beauty for the flight to death.

On the Bayou

The birds are bright as paradise at noon:
blue herons, cormorants, pink ibis, gulls.
With slapping sounds, two muskrats slip away
behind our wake. Some driftwood moves, alive,
and paddles near; a creature on the bank

begins to lumber down. The beasts make dull
officiants, half in hibernation still,
but hungry. Someone throws a fish among
the ripples; in a shine of hide, a flash
of teeth, the fish and alligator both

are gone. We float among dark eddies, bits
of spring debris, and silence. Farther back,
the thick, tenebrous recesses of swamp
inscribe a revery, the Spanish moss
and branches dangling in oneiric shapes,

the palms more beautiful than dreams. The light,
pale fingers through the cypress, and the wind
release the evening, and we leave, confirmed
in being, as it were, by sacrament—
a body sacrificed, a flesh remade.

Cattle Egrets

Blown here in the last century by storm
from Africa, they're immigrants, like us—
but they've adapted well to Texas, warm,
replete with fields and pastures, generous

in pleasure greens and fairways. Graceful, sleek,
they ride on cattle-back, and pick their meal
from hovering gnats and flies; or sometimes seek
along a tractor's wake their commonweal.

Their mores necessarily are their fate:
their own is all the company they keep;
they strut in an exaggerated gait,
move silently, and make their wingbeats deep.

Four city egrets, in formation, clear
a stand of nearby pines, soar upward, arc
as if for exercise, divide, then veer,
alighting in the woods of Hermann Park.

The reasons for such sallies are obscure.
Are insects swarming yonder in the lee
of weather? Does tall grass provide a lure,
lawn freshly-mown or newly-planted tree?

Their motive surely cannot be caprice—
they've such direction! In their purposed flight
I find both proper tension and release,
winged image of exertion at its height.

→

See, handsome creatures, how you are admired
as kin, though you hear instinct's call alone,
without the love by which a heart is fired,
the blade of knowledge lying next to bone.

Geese

In sky of oyster shell—the waning year's
pale composition of iron clouds and sun—
the geese fly south, a wedge that rises, veers
and falls, then spreads, the narrow V undone.

I'm migrating with them beside the fields
of rice in stubble and dry winter ground,
amazed, as desiccated affect yields
to once-familiar love, grown distant, found

again. In vectored harmony, they cruise—
each bird intent in being and in flight—
so different from a heart's inconstant ruse,
like oil on water, shifting in the light.

They bank on currents I cannot divine,
except by their trajectory; banal,
these waves of feeling, vindicating mine,
afford my act love's human rationale.

Climbing

—Big Bend, Texas

This is my place—a few red Herefords
grazing by a draw, and hills in flocks
displaying their rough flanks. Halfway
up I scan the land, following the skyline
in familiar arcs from Paisano northward
round the Davis Mountains; to the south,

Cathedral Peak and the Del Norte range.
Thunderheads collect and scale the blue.
Caliche and loose rock grate underfoot,
a graveyard habit; but verbena winks
with violet blossoms, and, in the agave,
cactus wrens keep whistling. As at sea,

horizons waver; inside me, space unfurls.
Each time I take the measure of ascent,
I ride it, traveler of the mind, worn knees
aching, but the immensity a sort of grace.
Near the crest, where scattered boulders
make crude burial mounds, the currents

that had paused with me a moment whirr
again in helix motions, then bound past;
an insect scrapes the stone. A mineral
essence is distilled from earth, and sky,
and rocky self, the old world undulating
in the light; I picture ancient bones again

in flesh, the giants rising from primeval
dunes, their footprints fiery, glazing over
all our poor impressions, and the herds
of white-faced stars collecting, pressed
along the fences in the hieratic darkness,
coming down to pasture—coming home.

Chimayo

In the church at Chimayo,
the women are bending,
rounded and brown as loaves
of bread. Silence
ripples on the stones.
Slipping down their beads,

the litanies flow
past islands of votive light,
into a stream of shadow.
Theirs is the spirit
broken, the body
of need. On the hillsides,

grain is ripening now.
Think of them as a retablo,
the center radiant,
even the figures
at the periphery giving
the evidence of grace.

Raton Pass

Leaving the grasslands and volcanic cones that rise up
toward the Rockies from the Llano Estacado,
here I am again following the roping narrows of Raton Pass
en route to Colorado, watching twin rails keep pace
below, and admiring the sentinel blue spruce
patrolling on the hillsides. A secretary I remember
from New Orleans who'd had to come up here once
was amazed that I was not afraid to drive this highway

—and alone. That's the viewpoint of a Lowlander,
or one who doesn't know the lift that mountains
give to thought. As I sort out their folds, then glance back
in the mirror, memories come galloping along—
tangled lines, knots of regret, scars. *This time*, though,
thank goodness, I'm no longer by myself. To pick up,
as we have done, the past—in fact, not fantasy—
is more adventuresome than taking inclines, curves,

and horseshoe loops at sixty miles per hour. Exhilarating,
too. I love your life, in its trajectory—that existential
progress into being, strong and singular and sculpted
as a juniper that wind has carved into itself,
or torrents roaring over rock. Not just your *acts*, however—
not only patents, tennis trophies, math solutions,
genius at devising thinking things. Nor books read,
however numerous, well chosen—nor ideas becoming

→

music, nor applause when you cut the Gordian knot. Rather,
these are signs, the phosphorescence of your deepest
self, of the presence that surpasses what you've done,
the passage to the person.—We've reached the crest;
a sinuous architecture of descent unfolds ahead, protected
by the palisades and castellated mesa top of Trinidad.
It's smooth for us—fine road and arcs like birds',
your love parallel to mine, our direction set into the blue.

In the Garden of the Gods

Askew, but gorgeously, the great rocks stand,
slant back, or balance as the gods have hurled
them in their games—a lithic sleight of hand
from marbles, golf, or wagers, when the world

was young. It's almost paradise, this weald—
blue sky, blue spruce, and bluebirds warbling, two
atop the highest branches, others well concealed
within deep thickets, chirping, rustling through

dense-needled boughs of ashen blue, dark green,
then darting out to sing together.—We
are bridges crossing an abyss, the keen
reply to questions no one asked, a sea

of understanding; we walk here to prove
how precious is the feathered tribe, how bright
red rocks and azure skies—how wondrous love
can be, full vindication of the light.

In the Wyoming Range

—For Chilton, Maureen, and Olivia
—For Pat, also

We've pitched camp here in an alpine lea, accessible
by corrugated forest roads of steep persuasion,
taking us two dozen miles from the nearest highway.
We've got space, good grass and tiny flowers,
spindly aspen clustered like shy girls, some fallen
trees, a creek called Fontenelle, full, thanks to rain,
and thick, abundant forest higher, chiefly spruce.
Not a soul to bother us—the pronghorns at a distance

simply stare, and deer stay hidden in the thickets—
except perhaps the bear we spotted on a ridge
as he ascended from the river, having drunk. In fact,
he's not in search of human meat. There's sunlight
through the evening, long, since it's the solstice now,
Midsummer's night, the feast day (almost)
of Saint John the Baptist, whose gory head shone
on the platter as at sundown.—Our fire's going well,

giving birth to radiant coals, confined within a ring
of stones now heating, and we've got our pot
of chili and two bottles of red wine. The ground
on which I set my tent is level—just dried droppings,
bits of vegetation, not too many rocks. A good thing:
this camping life is really for the young; whereas *I*
must bring two sleeping bags (it's cold at night
up here), a pillow, face and hand cream of four kinds,

four vials of pills and vitamins, and (counting spares)
four pairs of eyeglasses! Yikes! And when I wake
tomorrow, I'll need to get myself well placed and kneel
before I rise, using arm strength also, clumsily.
So what? For me, the sky, deep blue with rags of cloud,
is lovelier tonight than ever—notwithstanding age—
because I've ridden through so many human
storms, and since, though superannuated, I'm in love,

and wisely, and can see in starry figures the completion
of our circle.— There is fullness in this empty
bowl of meadow, plenitude as in a life viewed from both
ends of our desire, sensible in hours and minutes—
sweet, irreplaceable confections—keener still
across its breadth, its whole trajectory. And everything
we've missed is vacuous—those other selves not
born. The breeze, which whipped the tent flaps wildly

as we set things up, has gone off to the willow beds;
with chili eaten but the wine not gone, the evening lolls,
then sputters out, its remnants—silver, rose, a touch
of green—at play above the crest like wakeful
children. In the fire, a log of ashes breaks, collapses.
No matter: moonlight, brightly dressed, begins to frost
the aspen tops and tease the shadows; from the heart,
a glassy feeling ripples outward, shining, lucid, smooth.

Fire Ring

We dug a pit, placed rocks around the rim,
collected firewood of piñon pine
and juniper—dry branches, long-dead limb—
then watched the kindling catch and poured our wine.

The conflagration in the west burned low,
as if confined along a slickrock ledge,
then leapt, inflaming cirrus in a show
of sanguinary feast at heaven's edge.

As, later, the declining umber light
succumbed to shadows in their cloak and hood,
we too observed an immemorial rite—
officiants at the sacrifice of wood,

with offerings laid out on heated stones,
in celebration of the common creed,
their primal warming reaching to our bones,
attesting to the fellowship of need.

The stars broke through the darkness with a splash
and formed into their frothy patterns, pinned
by north; hot resin crackled, and a cache
of piñon embers quickened in the wind,

and cast a spray of red, an astral spark
that seared my hand, a radiant insect's wing—
the evidence of living flame, the mark
of love transfigured and transfiguring.

Notes

"Breakwater." Bray's Bayou is one of the canalized bayous that thread through Houston.

"In the Hayman Burn." The name refers to the largest forest fire in Colorado history, located in the Pike National Forest, chiefly in Park County, west of the Front Range, northwest of Colorado Springs. The name "Hayman" is that of a site near Tappan Gulch, at the fire's origin. The conflagration was started by a Forest Service employee, Terry Barton; she later admitted setting a fire disguised in such a way that it would appear, she hoped, to be the result of an abandoned campfire. The moisture level was extremely low, as was well known, and the flames spread in a short time over a wide area. One explanation for her act is that she wanted to burn the letters of her boyfriend, against whom she had a grudge. Another is that she wanted to get his attention. She was convicted of arson and sent to federal prison; she has now been released.

"By the Black Canyon of the Gunnison." This deep and beautiful canyon is in western Colorado. The area is now a national park.

"In Unaweep Canyon." Unaweep Canyon is in the Uncompahgre National Forest in far western Colorado, southwest of Grand Junction.

"By the Conejos River." The Conejos, a tributary of the Rio Grande, is in southwestern Colorado.

"Wilkerson Pass." This pass, which is on the route of US 24 in Park County, northwest of Colorado Springs, affords a magnificent view of South Park—a wide natural basin—and the mountains beyond. The term *bayou* is used in the area, along with *creek* and *river*.

"*Éventail*." Stéphane Mallarmé (1842–1898) wrote numerous poems, mostly short, under this title. Méry Laurent (really Marie-Rose Louviot) was his mistress.

"The Trout." Stichomythia is the arrangement of speeches in drama by which alternating lines are pronounced by different speakers, more or less answering each other, creating an A/B/A/B alternation.

"Louise at the Piano." Fontainebleau, southeast of Paris, is the site of the American Conservatory, where Nadia Boulanger (1887–1979) taught composition and piano. Robert Casadesus (1899–1972) taught there before World War II and became its director in 1945.

"Carafes." The still-life paintings in question are by the Italian painter Giorgio Morandi (1890–1964).

"Marmalade." The name *Llano* (Spanish for *plain*) refers to the Llano Estacado, an enormous elevated plateau, in the Panhandle of Texas and eastern New Mexico. The Canadian River flows out of New Mexico across the Panhandle. Charles Goodnight, whose holdings were in that area, was the most famous of the Texas ranch pioneers.

"Madeleine Gide in Algeria." The information on which this poem is based comes from various sources, most available in translation: André Gide's *Journal*, his autobiography, *Si le grain ne meurt* (1920, 1921), his letters, and especially *Et nunc manet in te* (1947), the confessional text he wrote after Madeleine's death in 1938 and published later.

"Mina Loy in Mexico." Information on which this poem is based comes from Carolyn Burke, *Becoming Modern* (New York: Farrar, Straus, and Giroux, 1996). Loy, born in England, lived from 1882 until 1966; she died in Aspen, Colorado.

"D. H. Lawrence in the Hopi Lands." Information on which this
poem is based comes from Laura Adams Armer's *Southwest*
(London, New York, Toronto: Longmans & Co., 1935), and
Lawrence's "The Hopi Snake Dance," originally published in *The
Adelphi*, republished in *Mornings in Mexico* (New York: Knopf,
1927). In an earlier essay on the Hopi Snake Dance, Lawrence
expressed his disdain for the ceremony and the people who came to
watch it. But in the *Adelphi* account he eliminated the scorn and
explored the religious aspects of the dance. Frieda was, of course,
Lawrence's wife; Mabel was Mabel Dodge Lujan, or Luhan, and
Tony Lujan her Indian husband. The name "Lorenzo" was used
frequently by Mabel. Lawrence, it will be recalled, was tubercular.
The name *Chelly* has only one syllable, pronounced "shay."

Translations from Pernette du Guillet (ca. 1520–1545). Pernette, as
she is called, following sixteenth-century custom, is viewed as one
of the three most important women poets of the French
Renaissance. Her passionate love affair with Maurice Scève, the
author of *Délie* (an anagram for *L'Idée*) and the primary poet of the
School of Lyons, furnished the subject matter for most of her
poems, certain of which (including some here) were explicit replies
to his. The reference to R has never been elucidated. While they
both used stock Neo-Platonic and Petrarchian material, they were
innovative also. They are often compared to the English
Metaphysicals.

"Burning in Louvain." Information on which this poem is based comes
from Alberto Manguel, *A History of Reading* (New York: Penguin,
1996).

"Vaux-le-Vicomte." Nicolas Fouquet (1615-1680) was superintendent
of finance under Louis XIV. His dealings with financiers and his
own mode of management allowed him to make an enormous
fortune, part of which he spent on a splendid residence. Louis XIV,
alerted by others and jealous of a sparkling and lavish fête given by
Fouquet at Vaux, ordered him arrested in 1661. After a three-year

trial, Fouquet was sentenced to banishment, but the monarch changed the sentence to life imprisonment.

"Christ Pantokrator." The altarpiece described is found in the Duomo (cathedral) of Monreale, immediately inland from Palermo, Sicily. The Duomo dates from the second half of the twelfth century.

Lightning in the Heart:
A Postface in Prose

The following pages constitute a detailed account of the love story that gave rise to the poems in section one of *Breakwater*, as well as certain poems in section three. The two modes of expression shed light on the story differently, to be sure. Whereas the poems, in which experience is stylized and usually recollected in Wordsworthian tranquility, are autonomous aesthetic objects as well as vehicles of meaning, the prose account, though it likewise has obviously been shaped, is closer to the original experiences and is intended to convey a feeling of the *vécu* (lived). Readers are invited to appreciate the correspondences (or auto-intertextuality) between the poems and the experiences recounted here.

****

This is a tale of romance, a lovely and unusual romance, not without an element of the marvelous, like those charming beasts of legend, or an amiable *deus ex machina* appearing from the theatre wings. To prolong the stage metaphor, it includes what the French call a *coup de théâtre*—a dramatic, unexpected, though not unwarranted, event. It also includes, twice, a *coup de foudre*—a bolt of lightning, or sudden love.

On the next-to-last weekend of July 2007, Eleanor Beebe, a friend from Houston, emailed me in Colorado Springs (my summer residence after Katrina struck New Orleans, where I had vowed not to spend another summer) to say that someone had asked her for my electronic address. She was then traveling with her husband, and, to save time, simply forwarded the message, so that I could reply, should I wish. I did not, however, get her note immediately, for I too was away, but without laptop. My good friend of fifty years, Nancy McCahren, had flown out from South Dakota to visit me; she and I had driven to Taos, New Mexico, for a long weekend. When we returned, on Monday evening, we did not look at our email. That is because ordinarily I had no Internet connection in my condo-minium apartment and, instead, had to take my laptop to the lobby to use the wireless provided there. After our drive from Taos and a stop at a supermarket, we found going down a bother, preferring instead to put away our purchases and unwind. We had drinks and a quick supper and she packed her things, since she had a flight leaving at 6:30 the next morning.

Tuesday, we duly rose at 4:00 or so in order for her to get off by taxi. Normally I would drive my guests to the airport, no matter what the hour; but, still somewhat unacquainted with the highways east of the city—my mother's home town, but greatly changed from my girlhood—and unable to see very well in the dark (these old eyes!), I was leery of venturing out then. I dressed summarily, had a mug of coffee, and helped Nancy carry her luggage down and waited with her for the cab. Back in the condo, I had another coffee, then thought about what to do. I collected the sheets from her bed and her used towels, but, mindful of neighbors, still asleep at that hour, did not start the washing machine. Dishes from the previous evening had been done. I could have read, or returned to some writing, but for that, daylight is better. Likewise, it was too early to gaze at Pike's Peak. On a whim, I decided to try the Internet connection right at my desk, knowing that, occasionally, it had worked, probably because someone nearby subscribed to a wireless service. It connected right away—a good omen—and, except perhaps for a few hours, remained available until I left Colorado two and a half months later.

So here was the message from Eleanor, with the forwarded one pasted in. When I saw its address line—and, shortly, the signature—I nearly leapt out of my chair. *Levitated* might be a better word. For the person who wished to get in touch with me was my first husband, Patric (about whom Nancy had inquired—a bit of foreshadowing). He and I had not seen each other for forty-four and a half years; we had not spoken by telephone for forty-three or so; since then there had been almost no contact of any other sort, though in 1993 I had received the video tape of his retirement party (he was with Shell Development in Houston), and I had responded with a card and note or so (unanswered) and had sent him a few books—he is a bibliophile—from my grandfather's or Aunt Flora's collection. Somewhat later, again indicating that he was thinking of me, he had asked Eleanor to forward a copy of one of his piano compositions, to show me that he had not neglected the musical work begun long ago. Occasionally someone would write to say she'd seen him and his second wife at the symphony or opera, or a Rice University function; a newspaper clipping came once or twice through a friend, and a long article about him in the Houston *Chronicle* on-line edition reached me. I knew that he had a gentleman's ranch west of the city. That is very meager information for four decades and more. Here, suddenly, was his e-signature and the expressed wish for my address so that he could write to me.

Some divorced couples see each other often, especially if there are children; on occasion they arrange to live very close, almost next door. Others stay in touch at holidays or more frequently, even if they live at a distance. Some become friends; I remember two couples in Virginia who divorced so that each could marry the other's spouse, and all four remained (apparently) very close. In other cases, there is loathing. Hatred, even indifference, on Patric's part seemed unlikely, because of the tape and music; occasionally, also, he would ask these opera-going friends or fellow Rice alumni about me. But I had no reason to assume anything more than mild interest, less the expression of any genuine concern or sentimental feeling than homage to the past. Nor, of course, did the first email message suggest more; he had simply said, by way of explanation to my friend, that he wanted to ask a few literary questions. Why not? Literature is my field.

To say that the message thrilled me, sent me over the top, is not too much. It was a *coup de théâtre*, utterly unexpected, and a new *coup de foudre*, powerful and quick, like that when Patric and I first met, on the stairs of the Fondren Library at what was then The Rice Institute. Each time, lightning struck in my heart, a bolt, an illumination. Though ra-tional, Cartesian even, I am excitable; after all, I'm a woman and, to boot, a poet, accustomed to cultivating feeling. And I'm a girl at heart—aren't we all, even the aged, still young somewhere inside? Recall Meursault's mother in *The Stranger* by Camus; in the old people's home, she acquires a "fiancé" and they walk together holding hands. In short, I'm a romantic who controls her romanticism. ("Classicism is a tamed romanticism," wrote

Gide.) I'm quite capable of acting like a young thing who's been asked out by a handsome, personable fellow—as indeed Patric was and remains (and brilliant also).

It was not just girlish giddiness, of course. There were deep feelings for years, long unacknowledged but powerful anyhow. As the aunt of my friend Patricia Teed said, upon hearing what we think of as "Our Story," "The pilot light never went out." I had looked at the retirement party tape more than once, avidly, lovingly, but with bitter tears of regret over my loss; I had cast my eyes around during each visit to Houston in hopes that, even in an urban area of five million or so, chance would bring Patric and me together in the same restaurant or shop; when driving on I-10 west of the city, on my many cross-Texas journeys, I bought gasoline every time in the little town closest to Patric's ranch and hung around the convenience store, getting coffee, looking idly at maps, buying a candy bar for the road, casting my eyes about like a criminal on the lam—except that I *wanted* to be identified.

I answered the email immediately, explaining that the reply had been delayed by the weekend spent in Taos. Darkness still surrounded me, but in Texas, an hour later, people were up and about; Patric replied shortly, saying he was "running late" (I didn't understand, not knowing his routine—to be explained shortly) and he would write more, but wanted to know meanwhile whether I recalled the name of the Irish poet we took to dinner at the San Jacinto Inn in 1958 or so. Thus began an "Internet romance" (so to speak) that has changed my life, and his, forever. It is ironic that I, the semi-Luddite, who rejects lots of gadgets as unneeded and almost immoral—enslaving more than enabling—and tries to hold technology at bay, should be so indebted this time to its electric magic. Love's new logic is the technological; and while neither email nor, even less, cell phone texting can rival the love letters of the past (that flowing handwriting of the nineteenth century! or, in the twentieth, typed missives with errors and erasures!), they have acquired their own charm.

The reader will want to know (I hope) more of the background to this renewal of communication, and especially why the contact was broken in the first place—why our marriage failed, though we loved each other. We are not quite sure ourselves. True, we can identify certain problems and errors, whether causes, symptoms, or consequences. Patric says the root cause was his; I insist that the fault was mostly mine (and I'm right). However that may be, each long ago forgave the other for shortcomings and failures; we agree that recrimination is out of the question. At a dinner with an old friend from university days and his wife, we acted (as we are) so very much in love that the question was put to us directly: why did you split up? As if the scene had been rehearsed, we looked at each other briefly, then said in unison, "We don't know." But Patric, a man of science and truth (though of love also), offered some explanation, acknowledging that we were young, too young, and thus, when there were differences, career pressures, and conflicting aspirations, and when mistakes were made, we did not deal with them well. Though nothing was said about it during that dinner, long ago the question of children arose at the wrong time—Patric, who would have been an outstanding father, proposing that we have a child, just as I was at a very low point emotionally and trying to launch a new phase of my young career. That I refused the prospect of maternity then is one of my bitterest regrets. To deny one's husband a child, where there is none, is a very grave act, and I cannot justify it now. Yet I would not wish to be the new Sarah, starting over as a septuagenarian. I must remember the angel in Voltaire's witty, irreverent, and wise story *Zadig*. When so much has gone wrong and the hero, having been sorely tried, wonders why destiny is as it is, the angel explains that, although he cannot pull back entirely the veil of the unknown, he can offer *some* enlightenment about kismet (Voltaire did not think of it as "Providence"): if a house burnt down, it was so that a buried treasure could thereby be exposed; if a son died, it was because otherwise he would have turned out to be a parricide.

This is fable, though a wise fable, at least as wise as any other commentary on the ways of fate and men. Similarly, any "What if?" speculation of mine about "vacuous reality"—what could be, logically, but is not—is merely that, a groundless fantasy, an attempt at rationalization, and a very poor cover ex post facto for my selfishness; yet we cannot know that *some* truth might not abide therein. The best I can do now, forty-five years later, is to be grateful for the beautiful and talented daughter who was born to me after I married someone else. I should add that, in the early 1990s, after she reached the age of twenty-one and was in her senior year at the Uni-versity of Chicago, this marriage also ended in separation and divorce, though her father and I maintained friendly relations and for fifteen years I still acted as his amanuensis when I was in New Orleans. While the sepa-ration was caused by serious difficulties and not effected simply so that I could be free to travel more frequently—I am now incapable of such selfishness—it is interesting that it came about roughly when Patric retired from Shell and had the tape mailed, jarring my feelings; I thus became able to loiter at a gasoline station on I-10 in Texas at a time when he might have been thinking of me.

As it happened (to return to the background of the romance with which this essay is concerned), the career aspirations mentioned above led Patric and me to be on different coasts, he in California, I in Virginia. Bad, very bad. Again, though he too now blames himself, knowing he'd been warned and realizing that he should not have gone to the West Coast (he remained not much more than three years), the separation was mostly my doing, a result of giving in, foolishly, to flattery and accepting very bad career advice from two or three directions. What could have been mended, had we been geographically close, became much harder to remedy and, finally, impossible in the mental and emotional condition of doubt, dis-couragement, fatigue, depression to which each had been reduced. Oh, if I had gone out during the Easter break that year! But my mother, greatly distressed and giving in to wild imaginations, I fear, counseled so strongly against my going, and with such pleading—for reasons unclear to me now as then—that, though I rarely heeded her precepts, on that occasion I dared not refuse. Why did I not follow my instinct, as it were? Aunt Flora, whose understanding was broader than my mother's in most things, wanted me to go and offered to buy my cross-country air ticket. Or if only I'd returned to California that summer! And taken a job there for the following year! Ah, how history would have been changed (as Pascal wrote) if the nose of Cleopatra had been shorter!

Why did Patric write to me in July 2007, after virtually no contact for decades (even the tape was mailed by his secretary)? He now says that he'd thought of doing so earlier—for instance, to ask the words of "The Bandera Waltz," which I'd once sung to him. When he finally did so, the pretext was not flimsy: being half-Irish, he is genuinely interested in Irish poetry and hoped to find out whether, as he thought, it was Seamus Heaney whom we'd taken to dinner (as indeed it was). But he could have refrained from acting on that pretext. While I do not acknowledge the existence of another self inside (the Freudian unconscious, dictating to us what to do), the causes of our actions are sometimes unclear, or unspoken. Though he says he had nothing in mind beyond asking a question or two, I was *on his mind*, surely. There had been changes in his personal situation in the previous few years, also, that might shed light on the matter. He had survived a serious heart attack caused by thrombosis, to which he'd always been vulnerable; and, following a stroke that affected both her body and mind, his wife had become an invalid, close to helpless, residing permanently in a nursing home, where he then became accustomed to spending nine hours a day, starting around 8 A.M., seven days a week. (She had no other family.) Already, before the stroke, they had sold the ranch and moved into a Houston high-rise condominium building. For one reason or another, activities of the past had become impractical or impossible for Patric: tennis (he was a very good amateur player but has bad knees, bone on bone—and when, with his schedule, would he have fitted it in?), ballet and opera performances, dinner parties. His life was thus dreadfully circumscribed. Beyond the care he generously proffered in the nursing home, only reading—thank goodness for books!—and mathematics were available to him as distractions while his wife slept; and in his free hours, already limited, he had to do laundry for both of them, run all his errands, shave, shower, sleep, and eat. That would wear down a saint. Did these circumstances make him more inclined to think of me?

Our initial exchange was followed by another that evening and notes throughout the week. They were personal in the sense that he set out his circumstances, and I mine, but their tone did not go beyond cordiality; they could have come from any friend of long ago. Their effect on me was powerful, however. As I wrote to Patricia (who answered "No surprise there," alluding to sentiments she'd long been aware of), love blossomed in no time, from roots that were still alive, and with it, regrets, needs, yearnings, hopes. Hopes for what? That was not clear; I dared not imagine the future very precisely. Not wishing to assume too much, I trod carefully in all I wrote, fearing hot coals—better put, the cold shower of indifference or worse, offense. Not at all: Patric's responses were encouraging, as we shared information about careers, books, music, and, on my part, social and cultural life in Colorado Springs in the summer. By the end of August, I had ventured to ask for his forgiveness, and received a gentle expression of it, in terms that might have been taken, by one more assured, as an admission of love. Indeed, lightning had struck him also. Proust observes that knowing someone is in love with you produces either vexation or the opposite effect. Patric's affection, long stifled and forcibly pushed underground, was ready to come to the surface. Didn't "Alph, the sacred river" run, according to Coleridge, "through caverns measureless to man"? But Patric's river of feeling ultimately flowed not into "a sunless sea" but a *sunlit* one.

In late summer 2007 it happened that I was on the road twice, once by myself, another time with my friends Peter and Margot Fawcett, who'd flown from England and to whom I wanted to show various parts of Colorado and New Mexico. As readers of *Finding Higher Ground* know, driving leads, for me at least, to reflection; on western roads with light traffic, woolgathering can be done safely, and the vast skies call for digression, development, and expansion of thought, like clouds drifting and changing shape. Peter and Margot, who are lively companions, asked questions and commented on everything we saw and did. But in quiet moments, my thought could move freely back and forth over the topic and the person you can guess. On both these journeys I took my laptop, and where Internet service was available, I reported to Patric on the scenery, dropping a few hints on my state of heart, though not saying directly how much I missed him, how I craved his words, his presence. I mailed off a few postcards of mountain scenes he would appreciate.

The Fawcetts and I ended our week's tour with two nights in Taos. By that time, I was in a sorry state of nerves, from deprivation and intense, anxious desire to make up for the past and start anew with Patric. To approach that lovely old town, part Indian, part Spanish, part modern art colony, where even tourist accommodations are traditionally designed and beauty is almost everywhere, we crossed the high sagebrush plateau from the northwest, then the canyon of the Rio Grande, and shortly found ourselves in the shadow of the great blue Sangre de Cristo Mountains and among magnificent cottonwoods and blue spruce. I was sensitive to the calming influence, perhaps the inspiration of the site (the Taos Indians consider their mountains sacred). Fortunately, the Kachina Lodge provided Internet connection. Writing to Patric to report on our activities, I said little more, but took my courage in both hands and resolved to lay open my heart the next time.

We drove back from Taos on the 10th of September; the Fawcetts were to leave on the 11th (expecting—wrongly, it turned out— half-empty planes on that somber anniversary). Shortly after midnight on the 11th, I was at my laptop—with low light and the door closed, in order not to disturb the guests—making one connection (electronic or "cybernetic") intended to lead to another (sentimental), surely one of the most momentous of my life. After having written some about Aunt Flora, whom Patric admired enormously, I at last made what could be called a declaration of love.

This was a matter of great delicacy, to which I was not at all insensitive; on the contrary. I have said that Patric was married—to an invalid, to be sure, but still, his wife. Expressed in conventional terms, the situa-tion sounds awful; would you report it, as such, to your old-fashioned grandmother, for instance? Yet it has proven that of the dozens of people to whom this story has been related, including professional-grade Catholics, ordinary Catholics, a devout Anglo-Catholic, several other very conservative

Anglicans, liberal Anglicans, three Baptists, numerous Methodists, two Jewish friends, an ex-nun, assorted deists, agnostics, and atheists, and even a Buddhist, all have applauded, recognizing, doubtless, that the law was made for man and not man for the law; put differently, abstraction must yield to the concrete, the universal to the particular. "Love is good at any age," wrote one of these supportive friends. All must believe that someone so generous of character as to spend sixty-three hours a week at the side of a disabled, incompetent spouse—not because other help is unavailable but in order to provide company and reassurance—surely deserves to have, in those few hours remaining, some life of his own, some sentimental and moral support, some affirming of what and who he is. Or, to put it differently, like everyone, he needs and deserves to love and be loved. *Honni soit qui mal y pense.*

Perhaps a further word on his situation is in order, lest it be concluded that he is a man of two loves; he wants it made clear that is not the case. In California, in his condition of distress after our prolonged separation, he became involved with a woman who pursued him ardently. On the 7th of April, our wedding anniversary, he informed her that he wanted to break off their relationship and try seriously to mend things with me—as, presumably, could have been done. First burning her papers, she attempted suicide, nearly successfully, cutting her wrists *and* swallowing quantities of phenobarbital. She was discovered just in time. Testifying to her conviction that life without him was not worth living—was, indeed, impossible—the act effectively served as blackmail. He insists that he did not love her; but, having let himself become involved to the point where such a drama and its consequences became possible, he was caught. Thenceforth, his responsibility toward her, he believed, was huge.

That recognition having come about, he took the next step and, following our unfortunate divorce, married her. He was (to judge by reports), a loyal and supportive husband. The pair may have gotten along reasonably well in their quotidian existence—human beings can make many accommodations. As the Romantic poet Vigny expressed it meta-phorically, in "this prison called life," we create little gardens, trying to make ourselves and others happy. There was, however, dissatisfaction also in the marriage and, on Patric's part, unhappiness. The pair pursued common projects and activities, far more than many other couples do—building their ranch house and developing the property, raising dogs and sometimes cattle, traveling extensively, entertaining, playing tennis and running an annual tournament. Yet today, he speaks of his care and support for the invalid she became as a sort of "civil duty"—like that, I suppose, which leads a moral society to take care of its elderly, its orphans, crippled, criminals, and insane. In such cases, the greater the depen-dency—and the keener the acknowledgment of the errors that may have led to dependency—the greater the responsibility. Soldiering on for decades, and especially recently, Patric is, as you see, a very strong man, morally speaking.

To return to my declaration of love in the night of 11th September: those readers who remember making sentimental gambles—nearly every-one—will suffer with me as I say that the next hours were dreadful. (Even Patric knows about sentimental gambles; he now says that when he proposed to me—the first time—he feared rejection. Ha!) What did I have to lose? Perhaps nothing, but that was not my outlook. My mood altered between hope, quickly dismissed as groundless, and doubt, similarly dismissed as groundless, or nearly. (Torturers are said to torment their victims by alternating prospects.) Suitably, perhaps, Patric took a day to reply to the message, whether considering its import, pondering how to proceed, or weighing his own feelings (though I wasn't the only one who clung to words cast via optic cable from state to state). At last, his answer came. He recalled a love poem I'd written for him years before, spoke of "paradise regained," and added that he wanted to return my love.

How often does life offer a second chance in such matters? From that day on, our relationship has developed as both an old love rediscovered and a new one. We firmly established our reconnection, deepening our ap-preciation of each other, broadening our understanding, sharpening our sensitivity, expanding our joy. From August through October 2007 I wrote for Patric the poems that became "A Colorado Suite"; we exchanged many more messages (sometime in early fall he said there were more than 200);

telephone calls followed when I was in away without a laptop and then continued as a supplement to emails. I printed out many of his mes-sages and, when traveling, am never without two or three in my document holder. It was decided that en route back to New Orleans I would stop in Houston and spend three nights at a Holiday Inn. On the phone line we bantered about who was the more excited at the prospect of our meeting, agreeing then that we both anticipated it with similar desire and similar painful impatience.

Imagine our reunion after nearly forty-five years! The new denim shirt I wore signified the fresh departure. Waiting in the hotel room, I was rest-less—of course—yet confident. "What if he's bald and obese?" someone had asked, kindly. Well, he'd mentioned that his hair—black, thick, and wavy years ago—was no longer the same, being somewhat affected by his medications; *good, you've got hair* (though in fact it is not a requirement). Obesity didn't seem likely for a man who'd been on the tennis court so much and who was vigilant about his health after a heart attack. And he'd sent me a picture, taken in the mid 1990s, of himself, still a fine-looking man. Yet . . . Dusk came early that October evening, and he didn't reach the hotel until well after 6, having gone home at 5, showered, shaved, and dressed (in a cowboy shirt and jeans, to please me). For many minutes, I looked out the window nervously and, finally, glimpsed, or thought I glimpsed, his silhouette as he approached the hotel entrance. I'd left my door slightly ajar, meanwhile. Suddenly a man entered, rather distinguished-looking, with white hair, but much shorter than Patric. "Good heavens," I said to myself, "he's shrunk!" No, it was a neighbor, having mistaken my door for his. Then it really *was* Patric, and our first embrace, marked by sweet tears of joy, was a long, long one (he said later he was afraid he'd break my ribs).

That was October. As I write this, several months have passed. I returned to Houston shortly, then soon again. By early November it had been decided that I would settle here, and—chance acting for us—that very weekend a unit was announced for sale in his condominium building. A realtor showed it to me on a Monday morning—the day after his birthday—and I signed the purchase papers immediately afterwards. By early December, the deal was closed, and I was able to arrange, with what seems extraordinary speed, for a moving company to pack, load, and transport my belongings a week before Christmas. I sold books, gave away books, threw out books and countless sacks of other things, cast off furniture, lamps, and pictures, and otherwise prepared for a previously-unplanned move from the city where, with interruptions, I'd lived for almost forty years. Finally, I drove to Houston a fourth time and have stayed.

Patric remains dutiful to his wife in the nursing home; my presence will not, should not change that. In the hours remaining at the end of each day, we share dinner in my place, listen to music, talk, look at art books, and (readers will wonder) make love; today's mores and literary conventions permit me to add that our lovemaking is exquisite, "sweet and thoughtful," as I imagined in the poem "Olives" (at a time when there was none at all). Occasionally we see friends (in the post-Katrina era, I certainly have more friends in Texas than in Louisiana), or go out to eat or to the opera, ballet, or a film at the art museum. Along with reading, writing, and doing chores and errands (including most of Patric's), my daytime hours are easily filled, just as in New Orleans. *La bonne cuisine bourgeoise* has provided Patric with healthier meals than he got in restaurants and from take-out and prepared items; he shortly lost eight pounds, making his weight (if not its distribution) about what it was fifty years ago. He looks less worn than when we first saw each other, with a twinkle again in his Irish eyes; he hums, sings, tells jokes, invents new witticisms, and seems at ease. What he earlier termed, without bitterness, his "stoicism" has been superseded by a large measure of true contentment. As we drove home from the opera the other evening, in heavy rain, he said, relieved to reach without mishap the intersection of Fannin and Holcombe Boulevard (our neighborhood), "This is where we belong."

Quite so. We do not evoke the unpleasant aspects of the past, or rarely; flagellation is not constructive in any normal existence. This is our life now, the amazing product (we call it our "human miracle") of recent months and old years, first those together long ago, then the many more when we were apart. The misery that each experienced then has surely contributed to our immense gratitude at being happy now; I in particular had time and reason to deplore my errors and learn from them. We are not concerned with conventionality. As a wise friend observed, whereas we should do a great deal to satisfy our conscience, there is much less need to satisfy conventions. No formula fits all lives anyhow, and few are without messiness. (Patric wrote, "Our love never died; it just got messed up.") There will be no disagreements, no quarrels; we hold our relationship dearer than any other enterprise and will nurture and care for it as for a babe. Whether I'm here in Houston or away on a gig or a visit to Europe or in Colorado for a short stay—Patric wants me to take advantage of my Colorado *Himmel*—nothing will separate us, really, save death of the mind or the body.

Until then, wiser than before, with increased fortitude as well as greater understanding and love, we will each be light to the other, taking to the second power all good things we share. I think of the *luminarias* that the Fawcetts and I saw among a cluster of modest houses squeezed behind our Taos hotel—those small lamps in what look like paper sacks, arranged artfully along the walkways and on the porches, spreading their glow, warming the adobe, making a garden of light. If we could marry, we would—I wear on my ring finger a beautiful emerald solitaire as a sign of that commitment; but as long as Patric's duty remains with his wife at the nursing facility, so it will be. We will play the cards not as they were originally dealt but as the game has now evolved, after we have already wagered, played, and lost to fate more than once. We still have a great deal to lay on the table in this serious enterprise in which one's whole self, and that of a beloved other, are engaged.

****

The lines above date from the early months of 2008. Since then, cancer, added to her other sufferings, has carried off Patric's wife, and we have remarried. Thus, though most of the poems in section one either concern the distant past or reflect, if obliquely, our new relationship during the months while she was still alive and Patric took care of her, the section ends with the epithalamium poem celebrating our second wedding.

How we have circled around! Our circle, though, is a spiral, widening around the axis. This evening, from the windows of our Houston abode, I admire white birds making great curves against the pale-gold sky. On other evenings, fog drifts and settles, a gauzy veil not unlike that I discovered with amazement among the live oaks on the Rice campus (since my West Texas girlhood home offered no such trees, still less mantles of pearly mist at twilight). And sometimes, far to the south or east, where this tentacled city reaches down toward the Gulf, lightning plays, its tremendous energy flashing through the darkness the way Patric's love strikes in my heart, fiery, powerful, and pure.